TWENTY FIRST CENTURY

science

GW00500652

REVISION

GCSE Biology

Philippa Gardom Hulme

and

Jean Martin

OXFORD

UNIVERSITY PRESS

OXFORD
UNIVERSITY PRESS

Great Clarendon Street, Oxford OX2 6DP

Oxford University Press is a department of the University of Oxford.
It furthers the University's objective of excellence in research, scholarship,
and education by publishing worldwide in

Oxford   New York

Auckland   Cape Town   Dar es Salaam   Hong Kong   Karachi
Kuala Lumpur   Madrid   Melbourne   Mexico City   Nairobi
New Delhi   Shanghai   Taipei   Toronto

With offices in

Argentina   Austria   Brazil   Chile   Czech Republic   France   Greece
Guatemala   Hungary   Italy   Japan   Poland   Portugal   Singapore
South Korea   Switzerland   Thailand   Turkey   Ukraine   Vietnam

© University of York on behalf of UYSEG and the Nuffield Foundation 2006

The moral rights of the author have been asserted

Database right Oxford University Press (maker)

First published 2007

All rights reserved. No part of this publication may be reproduced,
stored in a retrieval system, or transmitted, in any form or by any means,
without the prior permission in writing of Oxford University Press,
or as expressly permitted by law, or under terms agreed with the appropriate
reprographics rights organization. Enquiries concerning reproduction
outside the scope of the above should be sent to the Rights Department,
Oxford University Press, at the address above

You must not circulate this book in any other binding or cover
and you must impose this same condition on any acquirer

British Library Cataloguing in Publication Data

Data available

ISBN-13: 9780199152360

10 9 8 7 6 5 4 3 2 1

Printed in Great Britain Bell and Bain Ltd Glasgow

Author Acknowledgements
Thanks to Barney for all the ideas and constructive criticism. Thanks to Mum for some of the puzzles, and Mum
and Dad for help with checking. Thanks to Catherine and Sarah for keeping out of the study – and to Barney,
Mum, Dad and Helen for keeping them happy!

Philippa Gardom Hulme B1–B6

Acknowledgements
These resources have been developed to support teachers and students undertaking a new OCR suite of GCSE
Science specifications, Twenty First Century Science.

Many people from schools, colleges, universities, industry, and the professions have contributed to the
production of these resources. The feedback from over 75 Pilot Centres was invaluable. It led to significant
changes to the course specifications, and to the supporting resources for teaching and learning.

The University of York Science Education Group (UYSEG) and Nuffield Curriculum Centre worked in partnership
with an OCR team led by Mary Whitehouse, Elizabeth Herbert and Emily Clare to create the specifications,
which have their origins in the Beyond 2000 report (Millar & Osborne, 1998) and subsequent Key Stage 4
development work undertaken by UYSEG and the Nuffield Curriculum Centre for QCA. Bryan Milner and Michael
Reiss also contributed to this work, which is reported in: 21st Century Science GCSE Pilot Development: Final
Report (UYSEG, March 2002).

Sponsors
The development of Twenty First Century Science was made possible by generous support from:
• The Nuffield Foundation
• The Salters' Institute
• The Wellcome Trust

THE SALTERS' INSTITUTE

Contents

---

*The OCR specification describes six Ideas about Science. (Details of these are in Appendix F of the specification):
1 Data and their limitations
2 Correlation and cause
3 Developing explanations
4 The scientific community
5 Risk
6 Making decisions about science and technology

Two different Ideas about Science are included in each of our Revision Guides: GCSE Biology, GCSE Chemistry, and GCSE Physics. You need to learn about all six Ideas. The OCR specifications show which Ideas about Science are associated with modules 1 to 3. The Unit 1 written paper, covering modules 1 to 3, assesses these Ideas about Science. You may be expected to use additional Ideas about Science in your coursework and the Unit 3 Ideas in Context paper.

If you are not using each of the GCSE Biology, GCSE Chemistry, and GCSE Physics Revision Guides, then you will need to other resources to revise all six Ideas about Science.

About this book

To parents and carers

This book is designed to help students achieve their best in OCR's Twenty First Century GCSE Biology examination. It includes sections on each of the areas of biology explored by Twenty First Century Science.

This book is designed to be used! Students will get the most from it if they do as many of the Workout and GCSE-style questions as possible. Many students will also find it helpful to highlight, colour, and scribble extra notes in the Fact banks.

To students

This book is in 13 sections. There is one section for each biology modules B1 to B6, and seven sections (7.1 to 7.7) for module B7.

Each section includes:

Workout

Go through these on your own or with a friend. Write your answers in the book. If you get stuck, look in the Fact bank. The index will help you to find what you need. Check your answers at the back of the book.

Fact bank

Each fact bank summarizes information from the module in just six pages. Don't just read the Fact banks – highlight key points, scribble extra details in the margin or on sticky notes, and make up ways to help you remember things. The messier this book is by the time you take your exams, the better!

You could try getting a friend – or someone at home – to test you on the Fact banks. Or make cards to test yourself. These could have

- a question on one side and an answer on the other or
- a word on one side and its definition on the other

GCSE-style questions

These are very like the module test questions. All the answers are at the back of the book.

In every section, content required for Higher level only is shown like this: H

Skills assessment: case study, data analysis, and investigation

Turn to pages 172–177 for a summary of essential advice on maximizing your marks in these assessment tasks.

1 Use these words to finish labelling the diagram.

cell   nucleus   chromosomes   genes   DNA

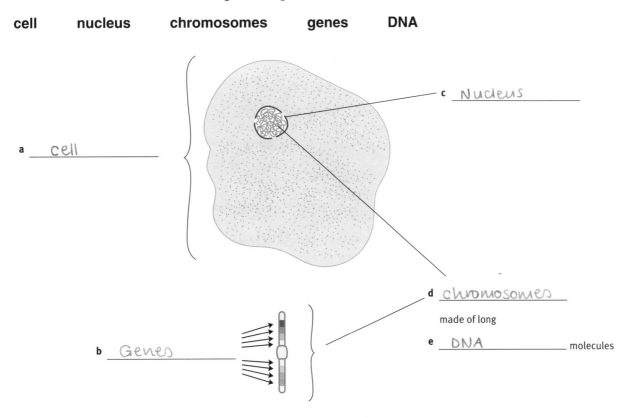

a __cell__

c __Nucleus__

b __Genes__

d __chromosomes__
made of long

e __DNA__ molecules

2 Write the letter T next to the statements that are true.
Write the letter F next to the statements that are false.

a Women have two X chromosomes in each cell, except for their
sex cells. __T__

b Men have one Y chromosome in each cell. __T__

c Human egg cells contain 46 chromosomes. __F__

d Every sperm has an X chromosome. Half of all sperm also have a
Y chromosome. __F__

e If a sperm with a Y chromosome fertilizes an egg, the embryo develops
female sex organs. __F__

f Your eye colour depends only on your genes, so eye colour is an
inherited characteristic. __T__

g You cannot influence characteristics that depend on both genetic and
environmental factors. __F__

h Different versions of the same gene are called alleles. __T__

3 Choose words from the box to fill in the gaps.

clones   genes   unspecialized   environments   asexual   sexual

Some strawberry plant cells are ___asexual ✗___ (*unspecialized*). These cells can

grow new plants. This is what happens in ___sexual___

reproduction. The new strawberry plants have genes that are exactly the

same as their parent's genes. They are ___clones___ of the

parent plant. In this case, all the variations between the strawberry plant

and its offspring are caused by differences in their ___environments___

4 Choose the best speech bubble opposite for each caption.

Write the letter of one caption in each speech bubble.

Captions:

A   I'm **h** the hairless allele.

B   … and me from Dad's sperm.

C   His ring finger is hairless!

D   We're both versions of just one gene.

E   Her ring finger is hairy!

F   … and me from Dad's sperm.

G   You'll always find us in the same place on the two chromosomes of a pair …

H   … Except in sex cells – each sperm or egg cell has only one of us!

I   Clare got me from Mum's egg …

J   I'm dominant.

K   So even though we've all got the same Mum and Dad, we're different from
each other!

L   … and me from Dad's sperm.

M   Joe got me from Mum's egg …

N   We go round in twos.

O   Naomi got me from Mum's egg …

P   Her ring finger is hairy!

Have you got a hairy ring finger?
It all depends on just one gene!

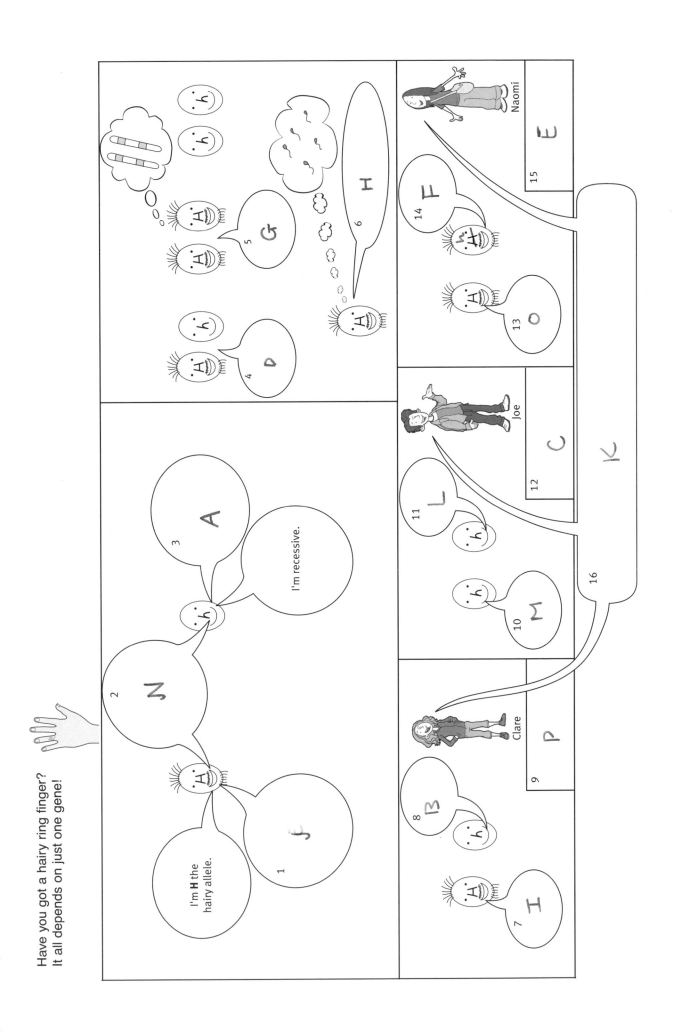

What are genes?

Every living organism is made from **cells**. Most cells have a **nucleus**. Inside the nucleus are **chromosomes**. Chromosomes are made from a chemical called DNA.

Chromosomes contain thousands of **genes**. Genes carry information that controls what an organism is like. Each gene determines one characteristic. The information in a gene is a set of instructions for making proteins, including

H
> structural proteins to build the body
> enzymes to speed up chemical reactions

Why do family members look alike, without being identical?

Human cells – except sperm and egg cells – contain **46 chromosomes**. The chromosomes are in 23 pairs. One chromosome in each pair came from the mother's egg and the other from the father's sperm.

In the two chromosomes of a pair, the same genes are in the same place. Often, the two genes of a pair are different from each other. Different versions of the same gene are called **alleles**. For each gene, a person has either two identical alleles or two different alleles.

A son shares some characteristics with his parents. This is because he developed from a fertilized egg that got alleles from both parents. Brothers and sisters are not identical because they have different mixtures of alleles.

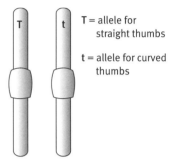

T = allele for straight thumbs

t = allele for curved thumbs

This person has straight thumbs.

> Some characteristics are determined by **one gene**, for example thumb shape.
> Most characteristics depend on instructions from **many genes**, for example height.
> Most characteristics also depend on **environmental factors**. For example, a man's genes may give him a high risk of heart disease. But if he has a healthy lifestyle he reduces his chance of getting ill.

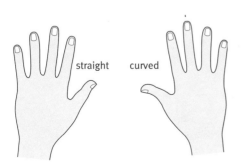

straight   curved

The allele that gives you straight thumbs is dominant. The allele that gives you curved thumbs is recessive.

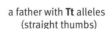

a father with **Tt** alleles (straight thumbs)

sex cells	T	t
t	Tt	tt
t	Tt	tt

a mother with **tt** alleles (curved thumbs)

There is a 50% chance that a child of these parents will have straight thumbs.

What makes humans male or female?

Humans have one pair of sex chromosomes in each body cell. Female humans have two X chromosomes (XX). Males have one X chromosome and one Y chromosome (XY).

Sex cells – sperm and eggs – contain only 23 chromosomes. The chromosomes are not paired up. Every egg has an X chromosome. Half of all sperm have an X chromosome; the other half have a Y chromosome. On the Y chromosome is a gene that is the instruction to make a male sex hormone.

At fertilization, a sperm nucleus fuses with an egg nucleus:

▶ If a Y sperm fertilizes an egg, the embryo develops male sex organs.
▶ If an X sperm fertilizes the egg, the embryo develops female sex organs.

What causes inherited diseases?

Huntington's disorder and cystic fibrosis are inherited diseases. They are caused by 'faulty' alleles of just one gene.

Huntington's disorder does not usually develop until someone is over 35. Sadly the disease is fatal.

Symptoms:

▶ loss of control over movements
▶ memory loss and mental deterioration

One faulty dominant allele – **H** – causes Huntington's disorder.

A person can inherit the disease from just one parent.

a father with **hh** alleles
(does not have Huntington's disorder)

a mother with **Hh** alleles (does have Huntington's disorder)	sex cells	h	h
	H	Hh	Hh
	h	hh	hh

There is a 50% chance that a child of these parents will inherit Huntington's disorder.

Children with cystic fibrosis produce thick, sticky mucus. The mucus

▶ blocks the lungs and air passages, making breathing difficult
▶ prevents enzymes getting to the gut, making digestion difficult
▶ encourages bacteria to grow which causes infection

A faulty recessive allele – **f** – causes cystic fibrosis. A baby who has two faulty alleles – one from each parent – has cystic fibrosis. A baby with one faulty allele is a carrier.

Carriers do not have the disease, but can pass it on to their children.

a father with **Ff** alleles
(carrier of cystic fibrosis)

a mother with **Ff** alleles (carrier of cystic fibrosis)	sex cells	F	f
	F	FF	Ff
	f	Ff	ff

There is a 25% chance that a child of these parents will inherit cystic fibrosis. There is a 50% chance that a child will be a carrier of cystic fibrosis.

How is genetic testing used?

▶ Some adults want to know if they are **carriers of a genetic disease**. Doctors extract genes from white blood cells and test them for disease-causing alleles.

▶ Doctors can take cells from a young fetus and test them for disease-causing alleles. If, for example, a fetus has two cystic fibrosis alleles, its parents may decide on a **termination**.

H ▶ **Insurance companies** could use genetic testing to assess the risk of a person having an illness. This is not allowed in the UK.

▶ Health authorities could test a whole population for a disease-causing allele. This is **genetic screening**. It is expensive, but may be cheaper than caring for children born with the disease.

Can parents avoid having a baby with a genetic disease?

Imagine one or both members of a couple are carriers of a genetic disease. They want a baby. They may decide to use the series of techniques below:

▶ Doctors use the father's sperm to fertilize eggs outside the mother's body (***in vitro* fertilization**). Embryos develop.

▶ Doctors test one cell from each eight-cell embryo for the disease-causing allele (**pre-implantation genetic diagnosis**).

▶ Doctors choose an embryo without the faulty allele to implant into the mother's uterus (**embryo selection**).

These techniques are not always successful.

What is gene therapy?

Scientists think some genetic diseases can be cured by gene therapy. Faulty alleles in cells will be replaced by normal alleles from a healthy person. This has worked for one disease, but not so far for cystic fibrosis.

What are stem cells? Are they useful?

Embryos contain **stem cells**. These are unspecialized cells that can develop into any type of cell. Doctors hope to use them in the future to treat some diseases.

What are clones?

Some bacteria, plants and simple animals reproduce asexually to make clones. Clones and their parents have **identical genes**. Environmental factors cause differences between clones.

Animals do not usually form clones, but there are exceptions:

▶ Identical twins are clones of each other.

▶ Scientists have made clones. They removed an egg cell nucleus. They took another nucleus from an adult body cell and transferred it to the 'empty' egg cell. They grew the embryo for a few days and then implanted it into a uterus.

1   Ellen and Hannah are identical twin girls.

a   Ellen and Hannah look the same as each other.
Choose the best explanations for this.
Put ticks in the correct boxes.

They have the same combination of alleles. ☐

They inherited genes from both parents. ☐

They both developed from one egg that was
fertilized by one sperm. ☑

They both started growing from one embryo.
The cells of the embryo separated. ☐   [1]

b   Ellen and Hannah look different from their mother.
Choose the best explanations for this.
Put ticks in the correct boxes.

A person's characteristics are affected by both genes
and the environment. ☑

They received alleles from both parents. ☐

The twins and their mother have different
combinations of alleles. ☐

Their cells contain 23 pairs of chromosomes. ☐   [1]

c   Ellen has one pair of sex chromosomes in each body cell.
Which two chromosomes are in this pair?
Circle the correct answer.

XY   **YY**   (**XX**)   [1]

d   John and Jim are identical twins. They are 50 years old.
John is fatter than Jim. Choose the best explanation for this.
Put a tick in the correct box.

They have different combinations of alleles. ☐

They are clones of each other. ☐

They have different lifestyles. ☑

John was born an hour before Jim. ☐   [1]

Total [4]

2 Complete the following sentences about genes.
Choose from this list.

**alleles   information   proteins   characteristic
carbohydrates   chromosomes   fats**

Living things are made from cells. Inside every cell nucleus are very

long threads called _chromosomes_ . These are made of

thousands of genes. Genes carry _information_ that controls

how a living thing will develop. Genes are the code for making

proteins . Each gene controls one _characteristic_ .   [4]

3 Complete the following sentences about stem cells.
Choose from this list.

**embryos   muscles   specialized   measles
unspecialized   research**

Stem cells are _unspecialized_ cells. Stem cells in

embryos can develop into any type of cell. Scientists

are doing _research_ about stem cells because it may be

possible to use them to treat some illnesses.   [3]

4 The allele that causes straight thumbs is dominant (**T**).
   The allele that causes curved thumbs is recessive (**t**).

   Sarah has straight thumbs. She has one **T** allele and one **t** allele.
   Alan has curved thumbs. He has **tt** alleles.

   a **i** What percentage of Sarah's egg cells contain the allele **T**?

   _____50%._____   [1]

   ii Give the number of **t** alleles in each of Alan's body cells
   (*not* the number in his sperm cells).

   _____2_____   [1]

   b **i** Finish the diagram to show which alleles Sarah and
   Alan's children may inherit.

   Sarah (mother)
   Tt

sex cells	T	t
Alan (father) **tt** t	Tt	tt
t	Tt	tt

   [3]

   ii Sarah and Alan have a baby boy.
   What is the chance of his having a straight thumb?
   Put a ring round the correct answer.

   25%   (**50%**)   **75%**   **100%**   [1]

   c Give an example of one human feature that is affected by
   several different genes.

   _____Hairs   on   fingers_____   [1]

   Total [7]

5 Huntington's disorder is an inherited disease.
   Its symptoms usually develop after the age of 35.

   a Give two symptoms of Huntington's disorder.

   1.) Memory loss

   2.) Loss of control of movement   [2]

   b Huntington's disorder is caused by a dominant allele of just
     one gene. The table shows the alleles of this gene in the cells
     of four people.

Name	Alleles
Abigail	Hh
Brenda	HH
Chris	hh
Deepa	hh

   Who will develop Huntington's disorder?
   Circle the correct name or names.

   Abigail   (**Brenda**)   **Chris**   **Deepa**   [1]

   c Gary is 20. He had a genetic test. The test shows that he will
     develop Huntington's disorder.

     i Suggest one reason why Gary may not want to tell his employer
       the results of the test.

       This may be a reason for him to

       miss out on a promotion   [1]

     ii Gary's wife is six weeks pregnant. Suggest one reason why the
        couple may decide to test the fetus for Huntington's disorder.
        Suggest one reason why they may decide not to have this test.

        For the test: to see if the child will

        inherit the disease

        Against the test: hard to kill the baby if it

        does have the disease   [2]

                                                   Total [6]

1 **a** Solve these anagrams:

   we sat   **sink**   **stare**   **a scotch maid**

   b Use your answers to annotate the picture to show some natural
       barriers to harmful microorganisms entering the body.

tears   skin

sweat   stomach
        acid

2 Write each phrase from the box in a sensible place on the
   flow diagram.

damage cells	**disease symptoms**
reproduce rapidly	**make toxins**

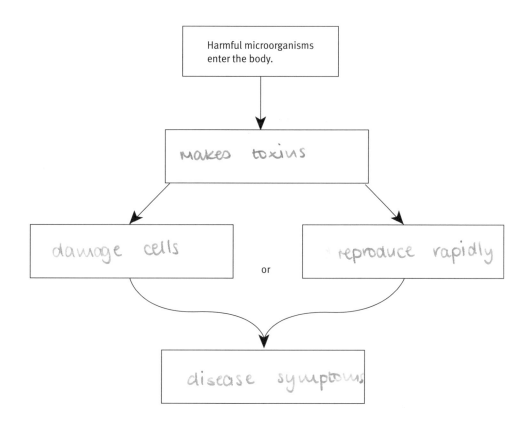

Harmful microorganisms
enter the body.

makes toxins

damage cells   or   reproduce rapidly

disease symptoms

3 The stages below describe how a vaccine works.

A The vaccine is made from dead or inactive parts of disease-causing microorganisms.

B White blood cells digest the clump.

C The vaccine is injected.

D When an active form of the same microorganism enters the blood, white blood cells make the same antibodies again. The microorganism is quickly destroyed.

E White blood cells make antibodies that stick to the microorganisms.

F The antibodies make the microorganisms clump together.

The stages are in the wrong order.

Write a letter in each empty box to show the correct order.

A	C	E	F	B	D

4 Here are the stages in making an influenza (flu) vaccine.

▶ <u>Experts meet in April to decide which strain of wild flu virus is likely to attack next winter.</u>

▶ In labs, scientists make a special 'hybrid' flu virus.

▶ This flu virus is delivered around the world.

▶ Technicians drill holes in fertilized hens' eggs.

▶ Technicians inject the flu virus into the eggs and seal the hole with wax.

▶ The eggs provide food and moisture. They are kept warm at about 37 °C for 10 days.

▶ Technicians harvest the flu virus from the eggs.

▶ In October, technicians break the flu virus into pieces and put it into the vaccine.

  a Underline the stage that takes account of the fact that the flu virus changes very quickly.

  b Draw a box around the stage that shows the conditions the flu virus needs to reproduce quickly.

  c Draw a cloud around the stage that shows how the virus is made safe before being put into the vaccine.

  d Draw a triangle around the stage that indicates that the flu virus spreads easily from person to person.

5   Write the letter **T** next to the statements that are true.
    Write the letter **F** next to the statements that are false.

a   Antibiotics kill fungi and bacteria. _T_

b   New drugs are tested for effectiveness on human cells that were
    grown in the lab. Then they are tested for safety on healthy human
    volunteers. _T_

c   New drugs are tested for safety and effectiveness on people who
    are ill. _T_

d   When drugs are tested on people who are ill, one group of patients
    takes the new drug. Another group of patients are controls. _T_

e   In 'double-blind' human drug trials, doctors know who is taking the
    new drug and who is in the control group. _F_

6   a   Fill in the empty boxes about the parts of the circulation system.

Part of circulation system	What does it do?	What is it made from?
heart	It pumps blood around your body.	Big muscle
artery	Pumps blood away fr. heart	Tubes. Thick walls. Muscle + elastic fibres
vein	Pumps blood to heart	Veins are tubes. They have thin walls made of muscle and elastic fibres.

b   i   What is a heart attack?

    A vein [artery] is blocked eg. too much fat
    resulting blood [oxygen] can't get to the heart.

ii   Your genes and your lifestyle both influence whether you might
     have a heart attack. Give three things a person can do to reduce
     their risk of a heart attack.

     1.) Not / reduce smoking
     2.) More exercise
     3.) Eat a healthy diet

How do our bodies resist infection?

Harmful **microorganisms** reproduce quickly inside the body, where it is warm and they have enough water and food. These conditions are ideal for microorganisms. They cause disease symptoms if they **damage cells** or **make poisons** that damage cells.

The body has barriers to microorganisms, including

- the skin
- chemicals in tears, sweat, and stomach acid

If harmful microorganisms get into the body, the **immune system** defends against the invaders. It tries to destroy them before they cause illness:

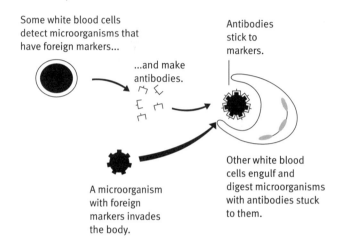

Some white blood cells detect microorganisms that have foreign markers...

...and make antibodies.

Antibodies stick to markers.

A microorganism with foreign markers invades the body.

Other white blood cells engulf and digest microorganisms with antibodies stuck to them.

Your body makes a different antibody to recognize every type of microorganism that enters it. Some of the white blood cells that make each antibody stay in your blood. So if a microorganism invades your body a second time, you quickly make the correct antibody. Your body is protected against that microorganism.

How do vaccines work?

Vaccines **prevent you getting diseases**. A vaccine contains dead or inactive parts of the disease-causing microorganism. After a vaccine is injected into your body, your white blood cells make antibodies against the microorganism. If an active – and dangerous – form of the same microorganism enters the blood in future, you make the same antibodies again. The microorganism is quickly destroyed. You are **immune** to this microorganism.

It is difficult to decide whether to have certain vaccinations. People must balance the risks of the disease against the risks of the vaccine's side effects.

H For society as a whole, vaccination is the best choice. A high percentage of the population must be vaccinated to prevent epidemics of infectious diseases.

Why is it difficult to make vaccines against some diseases?

▶ The flu virus changes quickly. There are many different strains of the disease. So new vaccines are needed every year.

H ▶ The HIV virus that causes AIDS changes (mutates) quickly inside the body. The virus also damages the immune system. There is no effective HIV/AIDS vaccine.

What are antibiotics, and how do they become less effective?

You cannot be immunized against every dangerous microorganism. Some microorganisms make you ill before your immune system destroys them. If the invading microorganisms are bacteria or fungi, doctors can often use antibiotics to kill them.

There are problems with antibiotics:

▶ Over time, some bacteria and fungi become resistant to antibiotics.
▶ You must take antibiotics only when necessary and finish all the tablets, even if you feel better.

H Random changes (mutations) in bacteria or fungi genes make new varieties that are less affected by an antibiotic. Some of the new varieties survive a course of antibiotics.

How are new drugs developed and tested?

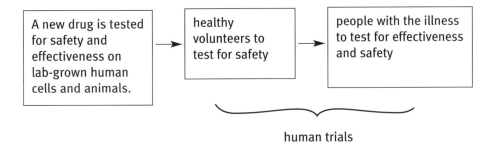

human trials

H In most human trials on ill people, one group of patients takes the new drug. Another group of patients are controls. The controls take either the existing treatment for the illness, or a placebo.

A **placebo** looks like the new treatment, but has no drugs in it. Placebos are not often used in human trials because people who take them miss out on the benefits of both new and existing treatments.

Human trials are 'blind' or 'double-blind'.

▶ In **double-blind** trials, neither patients nor doctors know who is in which group.
▶ In **blind trials**, doctors know who is in which group, but patients do not.

Why does the heart need its own blood supply?

Your heart pumps blood around the body, so heart muscle cells need a continuous supply of energy. This energy comes from respiration. Respiration is a chemical reaction in cells. The reaction uses glucose and oxygen. Energy is released. Blood brings glucose and oxygen to the heart so that the heart needs its own blood supply. Coronary arteries supply blood to the heart.

How does blood travel around the body?

Blood travels around your body through **arteries** and **veins**. Most arteries carry blood away from your heart. Most veins carry blood

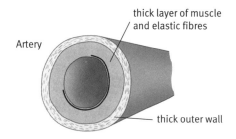

towards your heart. Blood vessels are well adapted to their functions:

Artery:

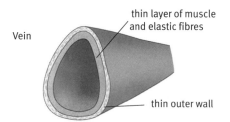

▶ thick, elastic muscular wall
▶ thin space for blood to flow through

Vein:

▶ thin outer wall
▶ wider space for blood to flow through

What is a heart attack? What factors increase the risk of heart disease?

Coronary arteries carry oxygenated blood to the heart. Fat can build up on the artery walls. A blood clot may form on this fat. This may block the artery. The blockage stops oxygen getting to the heart muscle. Heart cells die, and the heart is permanently damaged. This is a **heart attack**.

Poor diet, smoking, excess alcohol, and stress increase the risk of heart disease. Taking regular exercise reduces the risk of heart disease.

Heart disease is more common in the UK than in less industrialized countries.

1 a Catherine was coughing a lot. The doctor said she had an infection in her windpipe. He did not prescribe antibiotics.

Why might the doctor have decided not to prescribe antibiotics?

Put a tick next to the **one best** answer.

The cough was caused by a virus. ☑

She had not had the cough for very long. ☐

The cough was caused by a fungus. ☐

The cough was bad only at night. ☐ [1]

b A few days later, Catherine had a painful ear.
The doctor examined her and prescribed antibiotics.

i How did the antibiotics work?

Put a tick next to the **one best** answer.

They killed the virus that caused the painful ear. ☐

They immunized Catherine against the microorganism that caused the painful ear. ☐

They increased the resistance of the microorganism that caused the painful ear. ☐

They killed the bacteria that caused the painful ear. ☑ [1]

ii On the label, it says that you must take all the antibiotics, even if you feel better.
Explain why.

So that all the bacteria is killed, so
that the illness won't come back

[3]

Total [5]

2 a Which of these lifestyle factors increase a person's risk of having a heart attack?

Put a tick in **each of the correct boxes**.

a diet low in cholesterol ☐

smoking cigarettes ☑

drinking too much alcohol ☑

not taking regular exercise ☐ [2]

b Why do heart muscle cells need their own blood supply?

Put a tick in **each of the correct boxes**.

The heart needs a continuous supply of energy
to pump blood around the body. ☑

Heart muscle cells need a constant supply of
oxygen and carbon dioxide for respiration. ☑

Blood brings a constant supply of glucose and
oxygen to the heart. ☑

Each heart muscle cell has a nucleus that
contains genetic information. ☐ [2]

c The stages of one type of heart attack are given below.

A The heart muscle is starved of oxygen.

B Fat sticks to the wall of the coronary arteries.

C Part of the heart muscle is permanently damaged.

D Blood cannot get to part of the heart muscle.

E A blood clot forms on the fat.

The stages are in the wrong order.
Write a letter in each empty box to show the correct order.

B	E	D	A	C

[3]

Total [7]

3 Lauren has food poisoning. She has diarrhoea and vomits frequently.

She became ill after she ate a raw egg that contained *Salmonella* bacteria.

a Name one natural barrier in the body that could have prevented *Salmonella* bacteria entering Lauren's intestines.

_____Hydrochloric___acid___-_stomach___acid_____ [1]

b The graph shows the changes in the number of *Salmonella* bacteria in Lauren's stomach.

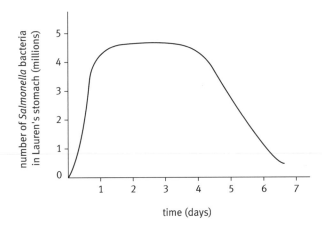

i Name the process that causes the number of bacteria to increase during the first few hours.

_____Reproduction_____ [1]

ii Use the graph to complete the sentence below.

Lauren will probably begin to feel better __4__ days after she ate the raw egg. [1]

23

c   Lauren's body tries to get rid of the *Salmonella* bacteria in two ways:

   ▶   Vomiting and diarrhoea remove some of the bacteria
        from the intestines.

   ▶   Certain blood cells can destroy the bacteria.

   i   Name the type of blood cells that can destroy *Salmonella* bacteria.

   _____White_____   [1]

   ii Suggest why Lauren's doctor advised her **not** to take
       anti-diarrhoea tablets.

   The anti-bodies in her body will
   concentrate on making the diarrhoea,
   go away rather than salmonella.   [1]

d   Lauren's doctor **did not** treat her *Salmonella* with antibiotics.

   Some farmers **do** give their chickens antibiotics when they
   are infected by *Salmonella*.

   Complete the sentences below to explain a problem
   this caused. Choose words from this list.

   resistant   mutated   killed   bacteria   viruses

   Some *Salmonella* bacteria became _resistant_____ to

   the antibiotic that farmers gave chickens. This antibiotic no

   longer __killed_____ the bacteria. So scientists searched

   for new antibiotics. But eventually __bacteria_____ became

   resistant to them, too.   [3]

   Total [8]

4   The graph shows the percentage of British 2-year-olds who had
    received the MMR vaccine from 1989 to 2002. The MMR vaccine
    prevents people getting measles, mumps, and rubella.

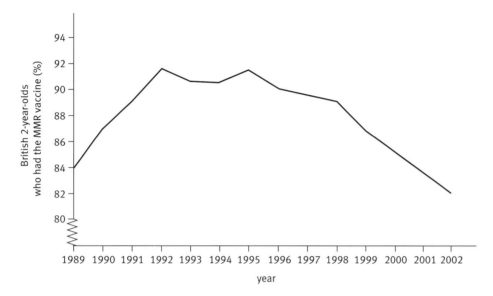

a   Here are some people's opinions about the triple MMR vaccine.

   A   I'm worried about the vaccine's possible serious side effects
       on my child.

   B   I'm a doctor. No vaccine is completely safe. The side effects
       of the MMR vaccine are a possible risk, but the dangers of measles,
       mumps, and rubella are worse.

   C   Measles is a nasty disease. I don't want to risk my child
       getting it.

   D   The more children who have the MMR vaccine, the better.
       Then everyone is protected from measles, mumps,
       and rubella.

   Use the graph and the opinions to complete the
   sentences below.

   Between 1989 and 1992 the percentage of children who had

   the MMR vaccine __increased__. One opinion that may explain

   this trend is opinion ___D___.

   Between 1992 and 2001 the percentage of children who had

   the MMR vaccine __decreased__. One opinion that

   may explain this trend is opinion ___A___.   [2]

b Matthew had the MMR vaccine when he was one.
Two years later, the measles virus got into his body.

Matthew did not get measles.
The stages below explain why.

A A nurse injects Matthew with the MMR vaccine.
The vaccine contains safe forms of measles,
mumps, and rubella viruses.

B Matthew's body makes the antibodies he needs
very quickly.

C The natural measles virus gets into Matthew's
bloodstream.

D The virus is destroyed before it has time to make
Matthew feel ill.

E Matthew's white blood cells make antibodies to
recognize the measles, mumps, and rubella viruses.

The stages are in the wrong order.
Write a letter in each empty box to show the correct order.

A	E	C	B	D

[3]

c Give one reason why a high percentage of the population must
be vaccinated against mumps to prevent a mumps epidemic.

So that the virus can't spread to
as many people.

[1]

Total [6]

1   Decide which statements are about natural selection, which statements
    are about selective breeding, and which statements apply to both.

    Write the letter of each statement in the correct part of the
    Venn diagram.

    A Individuals within a species show variation.

    B Humans choose individuals with the
        characteristics they want
        and breed from them.

    C Some individuals have features that
        help them survive if the
        environment changes.

    D The organisms that breed pass
        on their genes to their offspring.

    E Individuals with features that help
        them to survive live longer and so
        are more likely to reproduce.

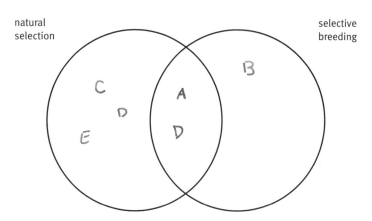

natural selection

selective breeding

C
D
A
E
D
B

2   Use the phrases in the box to label the diagram. You may use them
    more than once.

effector cells	receptor cells	neuron	central nervous system

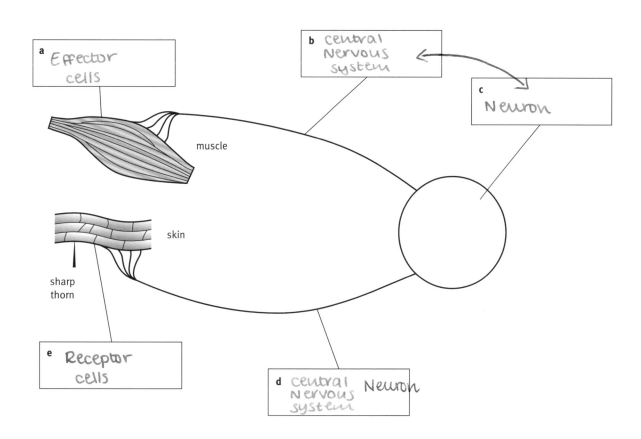

a Effector cells

b central Nervous system

c Neuron

muscle

skin

sharp thorn

e Receptor cells

d central Nervous system Neuron

27

H **3** Make notes about homeostasis in the table.

▶ Write a title in the top row.
▶ Write the two or three most important points in the next row down.
▶ Write other, detailed, information in the lower rows.

Title:	
Most important points:	
Other information:	

4 Do this activity with a friend.
Define the word at the top of the card. Do not use the 'taboo' words.
Get your friend to guess the word you are defining.

Hominid species	Mutations	Genetic variation
Taboo words: • human • big brains	*Taboo words:* • genes • changes • inherited	*Taboo words:* • characteristics • inherited • DNA
Competition *Taboo words:* • nutrients • water • survival	**Common ancestor** *Taboo words:* • descendants • related	**Multicellular organisms** *Taboo words:* • cells • many • plants • animals
Biodiversity *Taboo words:* • variety • species	**Sustainable development** *Taboo words:* • needs • future • environment	**Nervous system** *Taboo words:* • effector • receptor • electrical

5 Solve the clues to fill in the arrow-word.

Horizontal

3 The molecules that living things developed from were produced by environmental conditions on Earth at the time, or from elsewhere in the Solar . . .

7 All species of living things now on Earth . . . from simple living things.

10 Selective breeding . . . happens without the involvement of humans.

11 The molecules that living things developed from were produced by environmental conditions on . . . at the time, or from elsewhere in the Solar System.

13 The molecules that living things developed from were produced by environmental conditions on Earth at the time, or from elsewhere in the . . . System.

16 . . . is the symbol for the element oxygen.

Vertical

1 Nerve cells are also called . . .

2 Most scientists believe that life on Earth began . . . thousand five hundred million years ago.

3 Early humans with bigger brains had a better chance of . . . than those with smaller brains.

4 Mutated genes in . . . cells can be passed on to offspring.

5 Hormones . . . in the blood.

6 Living things depend on the environment and on other . . . of organisms for their survival.

8 . . . is the chemical that makes up chromosomes.

9 The first living things developed from molecules that could . . . themselves.

12 . . . is the symbol for the element hydrogen.

14 . . . is the symbol for the element carbon.

15 Changes that affect one species in a food web affect other species in the same . . . web.

1 ↓N	2 ↓T	3 → ↓S	Y	4 ↓S	5 ↓T	E	M
E	H	U	P	E	R	6 ↓S	A
U	R	R	Q	X	A	P	N
R	7 → E	V	R	P	V	E	8 ↑D
O	E	I	9 ↑	16 → O	E	C	D
10 → N	E	V	E	R	L	I	O
S	11 → E	A	R	T	12 H	E	O
13 → S	O	L	A	R	14 C	S	15 ↑F

How did life on Earth begin and evolve?

Life on Earth began about 3500 million years ago. Simple organisms developed from molecules that could copy themselves. Biologists disagree about the origin of these molecules – some believe that they were produced by environmental conditions on Earth at that time; others believe they came from elsewhere in the Solar System.

All species of living – and extinct – things on Earth evolved from the first simple organisms. Fossils and DNA analysis provide evidence for evolution.

What is evolution?

Evolution happens by **natural selection**. If conditions on Earth had been different, evolution would have happened differently. The number and variety of species that now exist may have been different.

The diagram shows how natural selection works. It is different from selective breeding, in which humans choose characteristics they want individuals to have.

Variation between individuals of a species is caused by both the **environment** and **genes**. Only genetic variation can be passed from one generation to the next, so without genetic variation there would be no natural selection.

Ⓗ Three things make genes change, or **mutate**:

▶ mistakes when copying chromosomes
▶ ionizing radiation
▶ some chemicals

If sex cell genes mutate, three things may happen:

▶ The mutation may have no effect.
▶ The fertilized egg may not develop.
▶ The offspring may have a better chance of surviving and reproducing. Then the mutated gene passes on to the next generation and becomes more common.

Over many years and generations, **new species** have evolved.

Ⓗ This is the result of the effects of mutations, environmental change, and natural selection.

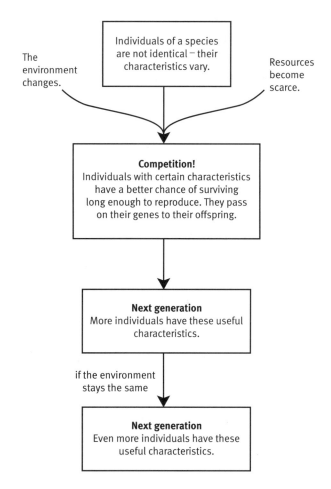

The environment changes.

Individuals of a species are not identical – their characteristics vary.

Resources become scarce.

Competition!
Individuals with certain characteristics have a better chance of surviving long enough to reproduce. They pass on their genes to their offspring.

Next generation
More individuals have these useful characteristics.

if the environment stays the same

Next generation
Even more individuals have these useful characteristics.

How did humans evolve?

Hominids are animals that are more like humans than apes. Many different hominid species evolved from a common ancestor. Those with **bigger brains** and who **walked upright** had a better chance of surviving. Gradually all hominid species, except for modern humans (*Homo sapiens*), became extinct.

How are human communication systems organised?

In living things with many cells – **multicellular organisms** – cells are specialized for different jobs. Multicellular organisms evolved two communication systems.

Nervous system

The nervous system uses electrical impulses to transmit messages and respond to them **quickly**. For example, you cough if you breathe in smoke and you blink if a fly gets in your eye.

In vertebrates, the nervous system is made of nerve cells (neurons). It is controlled by the central nervous system (the brain and spinal cord).

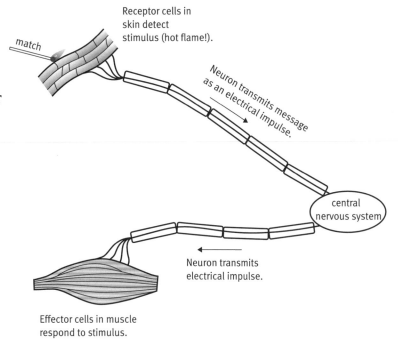

match

Receptor cells in skin detect stimulus (hot flame!).

Neuron transmits message as an electrical impulse.

central nervous system

Neuron transmits electrical impulse.

Effector cells in muscle respond to stimulus.

Hormones

Hormones are **chemicals** that travel in the blood. They carry information all over the body and bring about long-lasting responses. Hormones transmit messages more **slowly** than nerves.

Testosterone is a hormone. At puberty, it causes many changes in boys: the testes start to make sperm, the voice deepens, and pubic hair grows.

Insulin is another hormone. After a high-carbohydrate meal, the pancreas detects a high concentration of glucose in the blood. The pancreas makes insulin. Insulin causes the liver to remove glucose from the blood.

Homeostasis

Both the nervous and hormonal communication systems help to keep a constant internal environment in organisms. This is **homeostasis**.

For example, if you are too hot, the brain detects that the temperature of the blood flowing through it is too high. It sends an electrical impulse through the nervous system to your sweat glands. You start to sweat more.

Interdependence of organisms

Living organisms depend on **other species** and the **environment** for their needs, including nutrition and shelter. Within one habitat, species compete for resources. For example, in gardens, weeds compete with vegetables for light, water, nutrients, and space.

A food web shows how animals that live in a particular habitat meet their nutritional needs. It shows what animal eats what food.

Changes to one part of the food web affect other species in the same food web. For example, many foxes may get ill and die. The fox population decreases. The populations of foxes' prey species – mice, slugs, beetles, and frogs – then increase. At the same time, the badger population increases because there are fewer foxes to compete with for food.

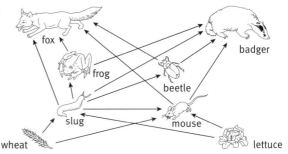

Why do some species become extinct?

Some species are extinct, or are in danger of becoming extinct. These changes may lead to a species becoming extinct:

▶ sudden changes in environmental conditions
▶ other species in the food web becoming extinct
▶ new species arriving that compete with, eat, or cause disease of the species

Human activity causes species to become extinct:

▶ Directly by hunting:
   – Passenger pigeons were hunted for sport and meat in North America.
   – Tasmanian tigers were killed by farmers whose sheep they ate.
▶ Indirectly by pollution or destroying habitats:
   – A cow medicine has poisoned and killed most vultures in India.
   – Pandas are endangered because their habitat is scarce.

Why is biodiversity important?

There is enormous variety in living organisms. This is called **biodiversity**. Biodiversity is important for many reasons:

▶ We may develop new medicines from species that we do not yet use.
▶ For new food sources: breeding cultivated rice with wild species may produce rice that is resistant to disease.

Biodiversity is an important part of **sustainable development**: using the environment to meet the needs of people today without damaging the Earth for the people of the future.

1 This question is about communication systems in humans.

a Complete the following sentences.

Choose words from this list:

electrical   long   short   slowly   quickly   chemicals   brain

The nervous system uses *electrical* impulses to transmit messages. It is controlled by the *brain* and spinal cord. Hormones are *chemicals* that travel in the blood. They transmit messages more *slowly* than nerves. Hormones bring about more *long*-term responses than the nervous system.

[5]

b Look at these examples of human responses.
Some are brought about by the nervous system, others by hormones.

Write the letters A, B, C, D, E, and F in the correct columns of the table.

A coughing when you breathe in smoke

B blinking when a fly gets in your eye

C controlling blood sugar levels

D developing breasts at puberty

E controlling how quickly you grow taller

F moving away quickly if you touch something hot

Changes brought about by the nervous system	Changes brought about by hormones
A B C F	D E C

[3]

Total [8]

2 Scientists have studied how 40 species of the cat family evolved. They discovered that lions and domestic cats shared a common ancestor 10.8 million years ago.

 a How might the scientists have obtained evidence to support their explanation?

 Tick the two best answers.

 studying fossils ☑

 analysing the fur of cat ancestors ☐

 analysing the DNA of modern cats, lions, and other species of the cat family ☑

 analysing the blood of cat ancestors ☐ [2]

 b i Complete this sentence.

 Domestic cats and lions evolved as a result of a process

 called natural _selection_. [1]

 ii The stages below explain how evolution made changes to one species: lions.

 The stages are in the wrong order.

 A More individuals in this generation had features that helped them survive in their new environment.

 B Early lions migrated from Asia to Africa. Some individuals had features that helped them survive in the new environment.

 C Individual lions are not identical; the species shows variation.

 D These lions bred. They passed on their genes to their cubs.

 Fill in the boxes to show the correct order. The first one has been done for you.

C	B	A	D

 [3]

 c The diagram shows scientists' ideas about when some species of the cat family began evolving from their common ancestor. For example, the domestic cat and the ocelot last shared a common ancestor 8.0 million years ago.

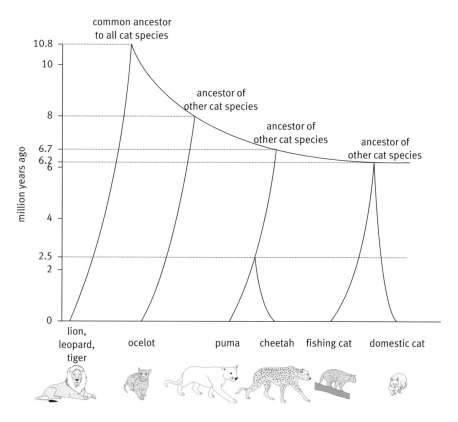

i When did the cheetah and the domestic cat last share a common ancestor?

6·7 million years ago [1]

ii Which species on the chart probably has DNA that is most similar to that of the domestic cat?

Fishing cat [1]

iii Read the information in the box.

> The common ancestor of the puma and cheetah lived in North America. Individuals of the ancestor species migrated. Some went to South America and evolved into a new species: the puma. Others went to Africa and evolved to become a different species: the cheetah.

Complete the following sentences. Choose words from this list.

mutations	survival	selection	environmental

This shows how _environmental_ changes help to produce

new species. Changes to genes (_mutations_) and natural

selection also help to produce new species. [3]

Total [11]

3 Read the information in the box.

Here is part of an Antarctic food web:

Scientists have discovered that the sea temperature around Antarctica has risen by 1°C since 1960. Warmer sea water creates problems for animals that live on the seabed. For example,

▶ scallops become unable to swim
▶ limpets cannot turn over

This makes it easier for predators to catch them.

a What is most likely to have made the temperature of sea water increase?

Draw a ring round the best answer.

acid rain   (**global warming**)   **the thinning ozone layer**   [1]

b i Use the food web to name one predator of the Antarctic scallop.

Brittle star

ii If the Antarctic scallop population decreases, what is likely to happen to the populations of its predators?

Decrease too   [2]

c Scientists fear that if Antarctic sea temperatures continue to rise, some species may become extinct.

Use the information in the box above to tick the **two most likely reasons** for the possible future extinction of the brittlestar.

Environmental conditions change.   ☑

A new species that is a competitor of the brittlestar is introduced to Antarctica.   ☑

Another living thing in the brittlestar's food chain becomes extinct.   ☑

A new species that is a predator of the brittlestar is introduced to Antarctica.   ☐   [2]

Total [5]

1 Next to each activity, write down one or more things affected by the activity.

Choose words and phrases from the box.

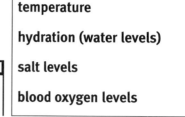

temperature

hydration (water levels)

H salt levels

blood oxygen levels

mountain climbing

living in hot climates

vigorous exercise

scuba-diving

2 Draw lines to match
   ▶ each part of an automatic control system in the body to its purpose **and**
   ▶ each purpose to a part of a premature baby's incubator

Part of an automatic control system in the body	Purpose	Part of artificial temperature control system in an incubator
receptor	to produce the response	thermostat with a switch
processing centre	to detect stimuli	heater
effector	to receive information and coordinate responses	temperature sensor

3 Fill in the gaps to show what enzymes do and how they work.

Enzymes are ___protein___ molecules that ___speeds___ ___up___ chemical reactions in cells.

Enzymes work best at ___37___ °C in humans.

   ▶ At lower temperatures, the reaction is too ___slow___ because
   ___there are less interactions with the molecules + enzymes___ .

   ▶ At higher temperatures, enzymes stop working.
   They are ___denatured___ .

   H This happens because ___the active site changes shape and so the___
   ___molecule can't fit the enzyme___ .

Every type of enzyme has a particular shape and speeds up a particular reaction. The molecules that take part in the reaction must be shaped to fit the enzyme's shape. The molecules bind to the enzyme at the ___active___ ___site___ . This is the ___lock___ ___and___ ___key___ model.

4 Look at captions **A** to **G**. Write one letter in each box to show what happens in each part of the body's temperature control system. Use each letter once or twice.

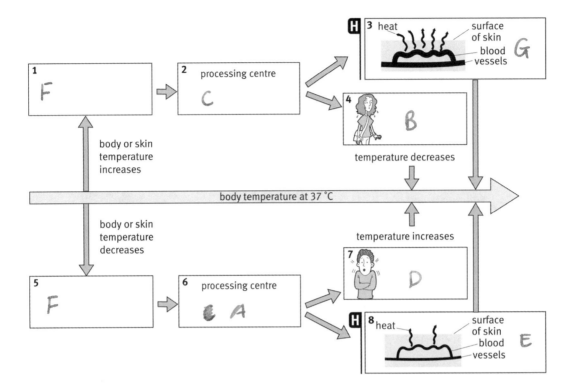

A ✓ The brain (hypothalamus)

 ▶ sends nerve impulses that cause muscle cells to contract quickly
 ▶ sends impulses to muscles in blood vessel walls

B ✓ Sweat glands make more sweat. Sweat evaporates, taking heat from the body.

C ✓ The brain (hypothalamus)

 ▶ sends more nerve impulses to sweat glands
 ▶ stops sending impulses to muscles in blood vessel walls

D Muscles in cells contract quickly. Cells respire faster and more heat is released.

E Muscles in blood vessel walls contract. Blood vessels get narrower. Less energy transferred as heat from body surface.

F ✓ Temperature receptors in the skin or brain detect this change.

G ✓ Muscles in blood vessel walls relax. Blood vessels get wider. More energy transferred as heat from body surface.

5 Finish the doctor's speech bubbles.

6 Finish the rescuer's speech bubbles.

7 Write **O** next to the sentences that apply to osmosis.
Write **D** next to the sentences that apply to diffusion.

Ⓗ Write **A** next to the sentences that apply to active transport.

You may write more than one letter next to a sentence.

a This process does not need energy.   D,O ✓

b In this process, liquid or gas molecules move
from an area of high concentration (where there
are many of them) to an area of low
concentration (where there are fewer of them).   D,O ✓

c In this process, molecules enter and/or leave a cell
through the cell's partially permeable membrane.   A O α D

d Carbon dioxide leaves cells by this process.   O α D

e This is a passive process.   D,O ✓

f Oxygen enters cells by this process.   A O α D

g In this process, water molecules go through a
partially permeable membrane from a dilute
solution to a concentrated solution.   A α O

Ⓗ **h** In this process, molecules move from a region
where they are at low concentration to a region
where they are at high concentration.   A ✓

i This process uses energy from respiration to
get molecules across the cell membrane.   O α A

8 **a** Annotate the picture to show

  ▶ three ways that water enters the body
  ▶ fours ways that water leaves the body

Ⓗ **b** Complete the sentences.

  i If too much water gets into an animal cell,

  _____

  _____

  ii If too much water leaves an animal cell,

  _____

  _____

GENTS

9 The stages below describe how urine is made and removed from the body. They are in the wrong order.

   A The remaining liquid is sent to the bladder. This urine contains urea, water and salt.

   B The urine is excreted from the body.

   C The kidneys filter out small molecules (urea, water, glucose, and salt) from the blood.

   D The urine is stored in the bladder.

   E Molecules the body needs are reabsorbed.

Fill in the boxes to show the correct order.

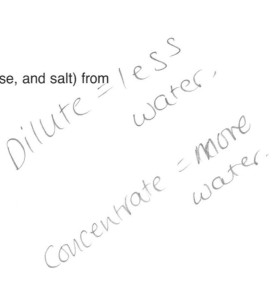
Dilute = less water, Concentrate = more water.

C	A	D	E	B

E A D B

10 Write **T** next to the sentences that are true.
Write **F** next to the sentences that are false.

   a The kidneys filter small molecules out of the blood.   T ✓ T

   b After exercise your kidneys make less urine than if you had not exercised. *Sweating = less urine*   F ✗ T

   c The kidneys reabsorb all the glucose back into the blood.   T ✓ T

   d Drinking alcohol makes a person's urine more diluted than normal.   F ✗ T

   e The kidneys reabsorb all the salt back into the blood.   F ✓ F

   f Drinking alcohol makes a person excrete a smaller volume of urine than normal.   T ✗ F

   g On hot days, your kidneys make more urine than on cold days.   F ✓ F

   h Taking Ecstasy leads to concentrated urine.   F ✗ F

   i After taking Ecstasy, a smaller volume of urine is made.   T ✓ T

   j Taking Ecstasy stops the pituitary gland releasing ADH.   T ✗ F

   k Alcohol makes the pituitary gland release more ADH.   F ✓ F

H **11** Look at captions **A** to **L** below. Write one letter in each box to show how water balance is controlled in the body.

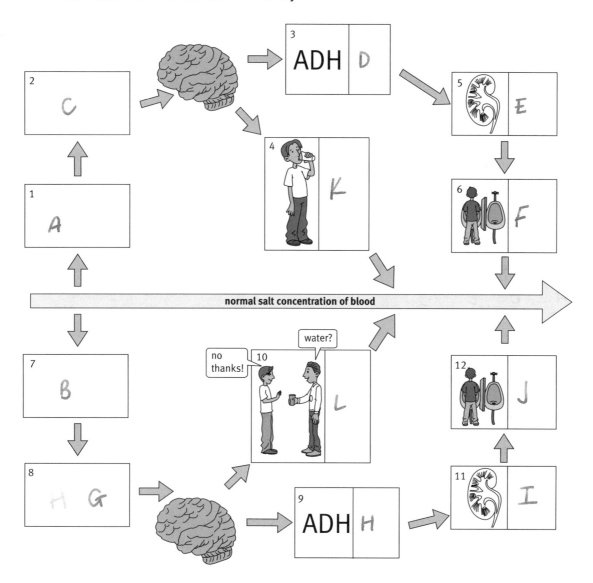

A The concentration of salt in the blood increases.

B The concentration of salt in the blood decreases.

C Receptors in the brain's hypothalamus detect that salt concentrations are too high.

D The hypothalamus causes the pituitary gland to release the hormone ADH into the blood stream.

E The ADH travels in the blood to the kidneys. More water is reabsorbed.

F Less urine is made. It is more concentrated.

G Receptors in the brain's hypothalamus detect that salt concentrations are too low.

H The hypothalamus causes the pituitary gland to release less ADH into the blood stream.

I The ADH travels to tubules in the kidneys. Less water is reabsorbed.

J More urine is made. It is more diluted.

K The person feels thirsty and drinks water.

L The person does not feel thirsty and drinks less water.

What is homeostasis?

Cells work properly only if conditions are correct, like temperature and water level. Automatic control systems keep body conditions constant. Keeping a constant internal environment is called **homeostasis**.

Body control systems are similar to artificial control systems. They have

- **receptors** to detect stimuli
- **processing centres** to receive information and coordinate responses
- **effectors** to produce responses

A baby incubator is an artificial control system. It has a temperature sensor, a thermostat with a switch, and a heater.

- The sensor detects the temperature. If it is cooler than 32 °C, the thermostat switches on the heater.

- The thermostat switches off the heater when the temperature rises back to 32 °C.

H In a control system, any change leads to an action that reverses the change. **Negative feedback** between the effector and the receptor makes this happen.

H Some effectors have opposite effects to each other. They work **antagonistically**. This makes the response very sensitive.

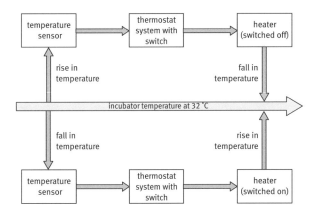

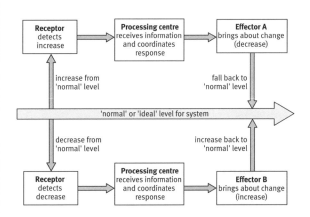

The table shows how activities affect homeostasis.

Activity	What it affects
strenuous exercise	temperature, hydration (water levels), H salt levels, H blood oxygen levels
surviving in hot or cold climates	temperature, hydration, H salt levels
H scuba diving	blood oxygen levels
mountain climbing	blood oxygen levels

Enzymes

Enzymes speed up chemical reactions in cells. Enzymes work best in certain conditions. This is an important reason for keeping cell conditions constant.

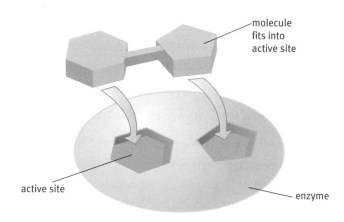

molecule fits into active site

active site

enzyme

Enzymes are protein molecules. Every type of enzyme has a different shape and speeds up a particular reaction. The molecules that take part in the reaction must fit exactly into the enzyme's **active site**. This is the **lock and key model**.

Enzymes in humans work best at 37 °C.

▸ Below 37 °C there are few collisions between enzyme molecules and reacting molecules. Reactions are too slow.

▸ At 37 °C collisions happen more often. Collisions also have more energy. So the reaction is faster.

▸ Above 37 °C, enzymes don't work. They **denature**.

H When an enzyme denatures the shape of the active site changes. Molecules no longer fit into the active site, so the reaction cannot happen. Changes in pH cause the same problem.

Keeping body temperature constant

Your body temperature must stay at 37 °C. **Respiration** releases energy from your food for your body to use. You may also gain energy from your environment, if it is hotter than you. Your body must balance energy gain and energy loss to keep a constant temperature.

The body's **core** is warmer than its **extremities** (for example hands and feet). At the core, energy is transferred to the blood. At the extremities, blood transfers energy to tissues.

The body's temperature control system includes

▸ temperature receptors in the skin to detect the temperature outside the body

▸ temperature receptors in the brain to detect the blood's temperature (**H** in the hypothalamus)

▸ a processing centre in the brain (**H** in the hypothalamus) which receives information from receptors and triggers responses in effectors

▸ effectors, for example sweat glands and muscles

At high body temperatures, the body cools down by

▸ making **sweat**. When sweat evaporates, energy is transferred from skin to sweat.

H ▸ **vasodilation**. Blood vessels that supply the skin's capillaries get wider. So more blood flows through the capillaries and the body loses more energy.

At low body temperatures, the body warms up by

▶ **shivering**, which happens when muscles contract fast. Respiration in the muscle cells increases. Respiration releases some energy as heat to nearby tissues. — cold

H ▶ **vasoconstriction**. Blood vessels that supply the skin's capillaries get narrower. So less blood flows through the capillaries and the body loses less energy.

Vasodilation and vasoconstriction are examples of effectors that work **antagonistically** (they are opposites). Their response is very sensitive.

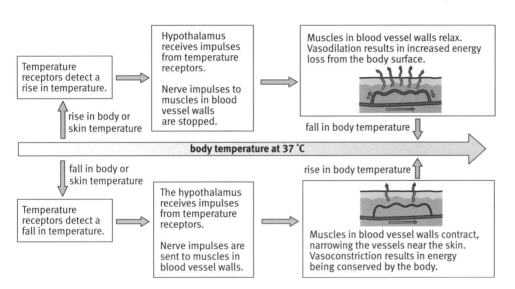

Heat stroke and hypothermia

	Heat stroke	Hypothermia
What is it?	when core body temperature rises above 42 °C	when core body temperature falls below 35 °C
Symptoms and causes	▶ hot, dry skin because sweating stops ▶ fast pulse rate because of dehydration and stress ▶ dizziness and confusion because nerve cells in the brain are damaged	▶ shivering, confusion, slurred speech, loss of co-ordination ▶ coma below 30 °C ▶ death below 28 °C
Treatment	▶ sponge with water ▶ put near a fan ▶ put ice under arms and in groin	▶ insulate the patient ▶ warm gently with warm towels ▶ give warm drinks
Other points	When it is very hot, you sweat more. This may cause dehydration. When you're dehydrated you sweat less, so your body temperature rises out of control. The body's normal methods of temperature control no longer work.	body loses energy faster than it gains energy

Getting substances into and out of cells

Liquid and gas molecules move randomly all the time. Overall, they move from an area of high concentration (where there are many of them) to an area of low concentration (where there are fewer of them). This is **diffusion**. It is a **passive** process – it does not need energy.

Cell membranes are **partially permeable**. Water molecules can get through their small holes. Overall, more water molecules diffuse through partially permeable membranes from a diluted solution (with many water molecules) to a more concentrated solution (with fewer water molecules). This is **osmosis**. ⟶ only water

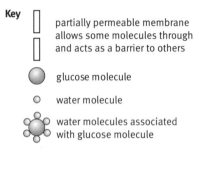

Key

▯ partially permeable membrane allows some molecules through and acts as a barrier to others

◯ glucose molecule

∘ water molecule

✾ water molecules associated with glucose molecule

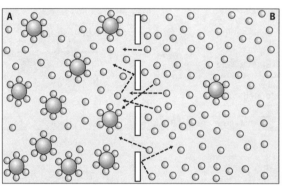

Overall, water molecules move from right (B) to left (A). This is osmosis.

Other chemicals (such as carbon dioxide, oxygen, and dissolved food molecules) also diffuse through partially permeable cell membranes.

H Sometimes a cell needs to take in molecules (such as glucose) that have a higher concentration inside the cell than outside it. The cell uses **active transport** to do this. Respiration provides energy for active transport.

Low - high

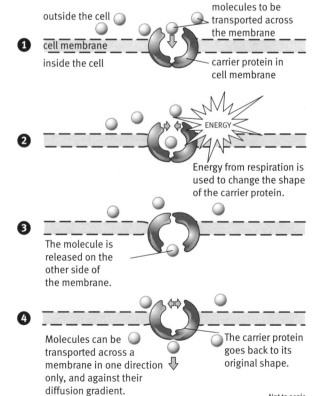

outside the cell

❶ cell membrane
inside the cell

molecules to be transported across the membrane

carrier protein in cell membrane

❷ ENERGY

Energy from respiration is used to change the shape of the carrier protein.

❸ The molecule is released on the other side of the membrane.

❹ Molecules can be transported across a membrane in one direction only, and against their diffusion gradient.

The carrier protein goes back to its original shape.

How molecules are moved across a cell membrane by active transport.

Not to scale

Controlling water levels

Cells only work properly if the concentrations of their contents are correct.

H If too much water moves into an animal cell, the cell membrane may rupture (break).

If too much water moves out of an animal cell, the solutions in the cell become too concentrated. The cell cannot work properly.

Water in
- food
- drinks
- respiration

Water out
- sweating
- breathing
- faeces
- urine

Your body loses and gains water to keep water levels balanced.

Your kidneys control water levels. They also get rid of waste products by **excretion**.

Kidneys work like this:

▶ They filter out small molecules from the blood (urea, water, glucose, and salt). Blood cells and protein molecules stay in the blood.

▶ They send all the urea, and some water and salt, to the bladder. This is **urine**. It is stored in the bladder and later excreted.

▶ They **reabsorb** molecules that the body needs – including all the glucose and some water and salt – back into the blood.

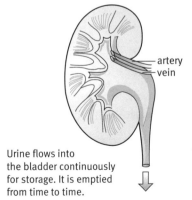

artery
vein

Urine flows into the bladder continuously for storage. It is emptied from time to time.

Cross-section through a kidney

Kidneys control water levels by making different amounts of urine. On hot days you sweat more. So your kidneys make less urine. You also make less urine after exercise, if you've not drunk much water, or if you've eaten salty food.

H Kidneys are part of a **negative feedback system**.

▶ **Receptors** in the hypothalamus detect changes in salt concentration in blood plasma.

▶ If salt concentrations are too high, the **processing centre** (hypothalamus) makes the **pituitary gland** release **ADH** (a hormone) into the bloodstream.

▶ The ADH travels to the kidneys (**effectors**). The more ADH that arrives, the more water the kidneys reabsorb. So the more concentrated the urine.

more ADH

more salt

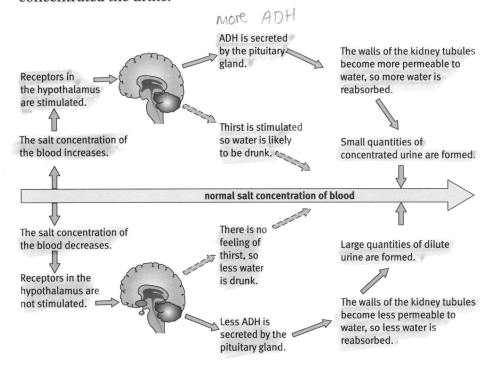

Drugs affect the amount of urine you make:

▶ Drinking alcohol leads to big volumes of dilute urine, so you may get dehydrated.

H This is because alcohol stops the pituitary gland releasing ADH. *– no feeling of thirst*

▶ Taking Ecstasy leads to small volumes of concentrated urine.

H This is because Ecstasy makes the pituitary gland release more ADH. *– feeling of thirst*

1 Premature babies are put in incubators.
An incubator is an artificial temperature control system.

a Draw a line to match each part of the incubator to the part of
the human body that does a similar job.

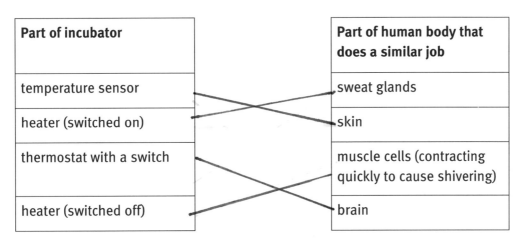

Part of incubator	Part of human body that does a similar job
temperature sensor	sweat glands
heater (switched on)	skin
thermostat with a switch	muscle cells (contracting quickly to cause shivering)
heater (switched off)	brain

[3]

b i A **negative feedback system** controls the temperature of
an incubator.

Which statement below **best** describes a negative feedback
system?
Put a tick in the **one** correct box.

If there is a change in the system, the system responds
immediately. ☐

If there is a change in the system, the system measures
the effect of the change. ☐

If there is a change in the system, there is an action that
increases the change. ☐

If there is a change in the system, there is an action
that reverses the change. ☑ [1]

ii **Antagonistic effectors** control the temperature of a human body.

Give **one advantage** of a control system having two antagonistic
effectors.

They are very sensitive

[1]

Total [5]

2 Catalase is an enzyme. It speeds up the breakdown of poisonous hydrogen peroxide molecules. The reaction happens in liver cells.

a What type of chemical is catalase?

Draw a ⟨ring⟩ around the correct answer.

fat   **carbohydrate**   **vitamin**   ⟨**protein**⟩   [1]

b Hydrogen peroxide molecules break down to make water and oxygen. The word equation for the reaction is below.

hydrogen peroxide → water + oxygen

Daniel does an experiment. He wants to find out how temperature affects the rate of this reaction.

He sets up the apparatus shown.

He drops a small piece of chicken liver into each test tube. Chicken liver contains catalase.

Frothy bubbles form above the liquid. The froth contains oxygen gas.

Daniel measures the highest point that the froth gets to after 30 seconds.

His results are below.

thermometer

water 30°C

water 70°C

ice and water mixture

hydrogen peroxide

Temperature (°C)	0	20	30	70
Height of froth (cm)	0.5	2	2.5	0

i Which of the following statements **best** explains why the reaction was faster at 30 °C than at 20 °C? Tick one box.

At 30 °C collisions between catalase and hydrogen peroxide are less frequent. ☐

At 30 °C collisions between catalase and hydrogen peroxide have more energy. ☐

At 30 °C collisions between catalase and hydrogen peroxide are more frequent and have more energy. ☑

At 30 °C collisions between catalase and hydrogen peroxide have more energy and are less frequent. ☐   [1]

ii Daniel saw no bubbles at 70 °C.

What has happened to the enzyme?

<u>   It has denatured   </u>   [1]

c Below is a schematic diagram of a hydrogen peroxide molecule.

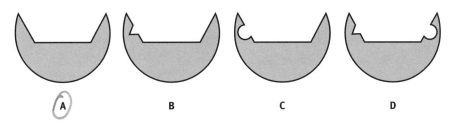

Which drawing represents the enzyme catalase?

Put a (ring) around the correct answer.

A   B   C   D   [1]

H **d i** Give the name of the part of an enzyme where reactions occur.

_____Active Site_____   [1]

ii If the pH is too high or too low, catalase does not speed up the breakdown of hydrogen peroxide molecules.

Explain why.

____The active site has changed shape, so__
__the molecule can't react._____

_____

_____   [2]

Total [7]

3

In 2003, a heat wave killed 30 000 people in Europe.

Many of the people who died were elderly. Scientists say that this is partly because elderly people are slower to detect high temperatures. So they are slower to do things that will help them cool down.

A person suffers heatstroke when the brain reaches 38.5 °C. The hypothalamus is damaged and their temperature control system fails. They no longer sweat and their temperature rises out of control.

A person with heatstroke has hot dry skin, a fast pulse rate, and is dizzy and confused.

Scientists advise preventing heatstroke by

▶ drinking lots of water
▶ staying inside at the hottest time of day
▶ getting cool at night
▶ avoiding alcohol

In another heat wave, in 2006, Italian emergency workers tried to prevent heatstroke by handing out water to people waiting in the sun for buses.

Doctors advise treating someone with heatstroke by

▶ sponging with cool water
▶ putting cool flannels on the face and neck

It is dangerous to throw lots of cold water over a person with heatstroke. This makes the body think it is losing too much heat, so it shuts down the circulation to the skin. That means that all the hot blood in the body is diverted towards the brain.

a Give **two** symptoms of heatstroke.

_____Dizzy_____

_____Confused_____ [2]

b Which part of the body's temperature control system works less well in old people than in young people, according to the article?

Draw a (ring) around the correct answer.

sensors   processing centre   effectors [1]

c Explain why drinking plenty of water helps to prevent heatstroke.

_____

_____

_____

[2]

d Suggest why cooling down properly at night helps to prevent heatstroke.

_____

_____

_____

[2]

e A person who has heatstroke stops sweating.

Explain why this is a problem.

One mark is for writing in sentences with correct spelling, punctuation, and grammar.

They ~~do not~~ are dehydrated, and so ~~its~~ ~~water can't~~ there is not enough to be excreted as sweat. ~~The hypothalamus~~ You don't sweat, so body temp. rises.

[2+1]

f i Which part of the temperature control system does alcohol interfere with?

Draw a (ring) around the correct answer.

sensors   **(processing centre)**   **effectors**

[1]

ii Suggest another reason why doctors advise avoiding alcohol to prevent heatstroke.

_____

_____

_____

[1]

H

g Explain why it is dangerous to throw cold water over a heatstroke victim.

_____

_____

_____

[2]

Total [14]

4 This question is about how chemicals move into and out of animal cells.

 a Name two chemicals that move into or out of animal cells by diffusion.

  oxygen   *carbon dioxide* [2]

 b **i** Which of the following statements **best** describes osmosis?

  Tick one box.

  Molecules move from a region of their high concentration to a region of their low concentration through a partially permeable membrane. ✓

  Molecules move from a region of their low concentration to a region of their high concentration through a partially permeable membrane. ☐

  Water molecules move from a dilute solution to a concentrated solution through a partially permeable membrane. ☐

  Water molecules move from a concentrated solution to a dilute solution through a partially permeable membrane. ☐ [1]

 ii What can happen if too much water moves into an animal cell?

  It breakes - ruptures [1]

 c The table shows the concentration of ions of two chemicals inside and outside a cell.

Ion	Relative concentration inside cell	Relative concentration outside cell
Na⁺	10	143
K⁺	140	5

  Draw a line to match each substance to how it gets into the cell.

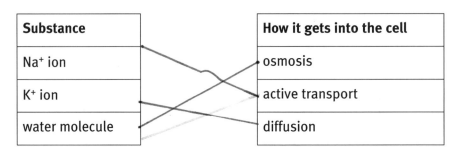

Substance		How it gets into the cell
Na⁺ ion		osmosis
K⁺ ion		active transport
water molecule		diffusion

[2]

Total [6]

1 Use words from the box to fill in the gaps.

DNA	genes	chromosomes	copied	double helix

Most cells have a nucleus. Inside the nucleus are __chromosomes__

These contain __genes__, which carry information that controls

what an animal or plant is like.

Chromosomes are made from __DNA__ molecules. These molecules are

very long. They are made of two strands twisted together in a spiral,

called a __double Helix__. DNA molecules can be

__copied__ very accurately because of this structure.

nucleus.
chromosome
gene
DNA
Bases

2 Look at captions **A** to **H**. Write one letter in each square box on the diagram.

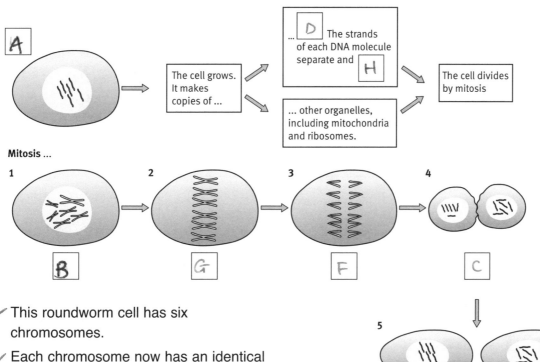

A This roundworm cell has six chromosomes.

B Each chromosome now has an identical copy attached to it.

C The cell divides.

D …its chromosomes.

E There are now two cells. They are each identical to the parent cell.

F The chromosome copies separate and move to opposite ends of the cell.

G The chromosomes, with copies attached, move to the centre of the cell.

H New DNA strands form next to each strand.

3 The flow diagram is about mitosis and meiosis in humans.

Use words and numbers from the box to fill in the gaps.
Use each word or number once, more than once or not at all.

fertilization	eggs	ovaries	testes	sperm	stem	meiosis
mitosis	zygote	2 4 8 16 21 23 42 46				

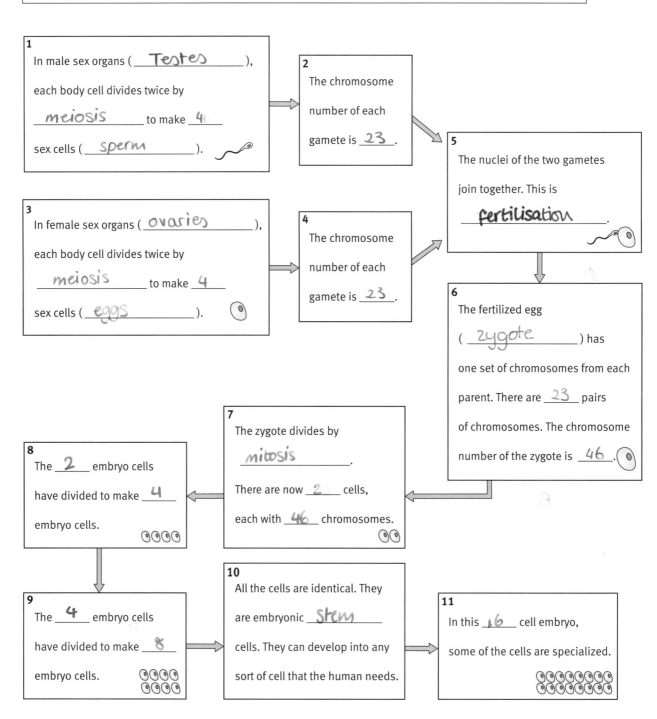

1
In male sex organs (___Testes___),
each body cell divides twice by
___meiosis___ to make _4_
sex cells (___sperm___).

2
The chromosome number of each gamete is _23_.

3
In female sex organs (___ovaries___),
each body cell divides twice by
___meiosis___ to make _4_
sex cells (___eggs___).

4
The chromosome number of each gamete is _23_.

5
The nuclei of the two gametes join together. This is ___fertilisation___.

6
The fertilized egg
(___zygote___) has
one set of chromosomes from each parent. There are _23_ pairs of chromosomes. The chromosome number of the zygote is _46_.

7
The zygote divides by ___mitosis___.
There are now _2_ cells, each with _46_ chromosomes.

8
The _2_ embryo cells have divided to make _4_ embryo cells.

9
The _4_ embryo cells have divided to make _8_ embryo cells.

10
All the cells are identical. They are embryonic ___stem___ cells. They can develop into any sort of cell that the human needs.

11
In this _16_ cell embryo, some of the cells are specialized.

4   Fill in the empty boxes to show the differences between mitosis and meiosis.

	Meiosis	Mitosis
What does it make?	gametes (sex cells)	cells the body needs
How many new cells does each parent cell make?	4	2
How many chromosomes are in each new cell?	23	same as in parent cell
Where does it happen?	in sex organs	anywhere
Why does it happen?	so reproduction	so an organism can grow, reproduce and replace damaged cells

5   This activity describes how a DNA molecule makes an exact copy of itself.

▶   In boxes **a** to **d**, draw a (ring) round the correct bold words or numbers.

▶   Draw lines to match each diagram **1** to **4** to the correct description.

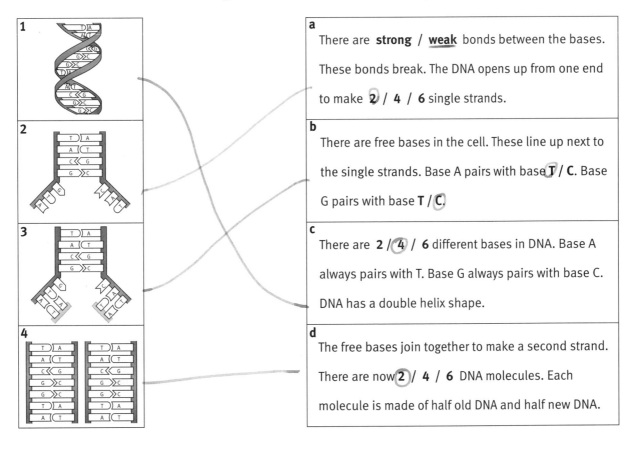

1

2

3

4

a
There are **strong** / **weak** bonds between the bases.

These bonds break. The DNA opens up from one end

to make **2** / **4** / **6** single strands.

b
There are free bases in the cell. These line up next to

the single strands. Base A pairs with base **T** / **C**. Base

G pairs with base **T** / **C**.

c
There are **2** / **4** / **6** different bases in DNA. Base A

always pairs with T. Base G always pairs with base C.

DNA has a double helix shape.

d
The free bases join together to make a second strand.

There are now **2** / **4** / **6** DNA molecules. Each

molecule is made of half old DNA and half new DNA.

6 Complete the speech bubbles to explain how and why stem cells are useful.

So why all this stem cell research?

Well, we reckon they could be really useful for...

Where do stem cells come from?

You can get them from early embryos, umbilical cord blood and adults. Embryonic stem cells are most useful.

Why?

Because...

But isn't that ethically wrong?

Some people think so, yes. Also, embryonic stem cell tissues don't have the same genes as the person getting the transplant. So...

What about therapeutic cloning, then?

Well, there's no problem of rejection here because...

What about adult stem cells? I can't see how that would work. I thought lots of genes are switched off in most cell. So adult stem cells could only grow into a few cell types.

True. If we could switch genes back on, we could use them. But it's really difficult to reactivate genes. The other problem is...

So has there been any success?

Some, we think, yes. We treated 60 patients with heart disease by injecting stem cells from a patient's bone marrow into their heart muscle. This worked better than other potential treatments. We also hope to use stem cell technology to...

7 Write the letters of the statements in sensible places on the Venn diagram.

A Grow in height and width for their whole lives.

B Contain organs.

C Grow only at meristems.

D Grow all over.

E Contain groups of similar cells called tissues.

F Do not continue to grow for their whole lives.

G Have organs, including leaves, roots and flowers.

H Contain specialized cells.

I Can regrow whole organs if they are damaged.

plants   animals

C
D
A   E
B
G   H   F
I   D

8 Draw lines to link pairs of words.

Write a sentence on each line to show how the two words are linked together.

unspecialized

identical   stem cells

asexual   cuttings

clones   rooting powder

meristem   auxins

roots

9 All the words in this wordsearch are about the growth and development of plants and animals.

> ▶ Find one word beginning with each of the letters in the table.
> ▶ Write a crossword-type clue for each word.

H	C	D	E	M	O	S	O	B	I	R	T	A	S	C
P	H	O	T	O	T	R	O	P	I	S	M	R	U	E
T	R	U	N	S	P	E	C	I	A	L	I	Z	E	D
I	O	B	A	S	E	S	S	E	U	N	T	T	L	I
S	M	L	H	A	M	E	L	Y	X	R	O	E	C	A
S	O	E	G	P	P	I	L	I	I	H	C	M	U	P
U	S	H	A	E	N	R	A	G	N	B	H	C	N	A
E	O	E	M	B	R	Y	O	N	I	C	O	E	M	Y
G	M	L	E	E	F	E	T	U	S	Y	N	L	R	A
H	E	I	T	T	A	K	D	O	R	A	D	L	W	D
T	N	X	E	E	T	O	G	Y	Z	E	R	S	E	L
J	Y	A	S	M	M	I	N	A	C	T	I	V	E	O
X	S	E	M	A	S	E	L	L	E	N	A	G	R	O

Word	Clue
A	
C	
D	
E	
F	
G	
M	
N	
O	
P	
T	
U	
X	
Y	
Z	

Making new cells

Living things make new cells so that they can grow, reproduce, and replace damaged cells. All new cells are made by **cell division**.

Making new body cells by mitosis

First, a cell grows. It makes copies of its specialized parts (**organelles**), including

specialized part of the cell, eg nucleus / mitrocondria.

- chromosomes, which carry genetic information
- mitochondria, where respiration takes place

Next, **mitosis** happens. In mitosis the chromosome copies separate and go to opposite ends of the cell. Then the whole cell divides to make two new cells. The new cells are identical to each other and to the parent cell.

mitosis = IDENTICAL COPY

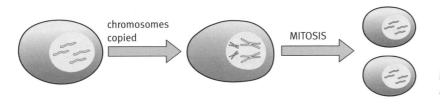

chromosomes copied

MITOSIS

Mitosis of a cell with 4 chromosomes.

Making sex cells by meiosis

Meiosis makes sex cells (**gametes**). It happens in sex organs. In meiosis, a body cell divides twice to make four gametes. Gametes are not identical – they each carry different genetic information.

meiosis = ½ no. of chromosome

Gametes have half the number of chromosomes as the parent cell. Human body cells have 46 chromosomes, arranged in 23 pairs. So human gametes (sperm and egg cells) have only 23 single chromosomes.

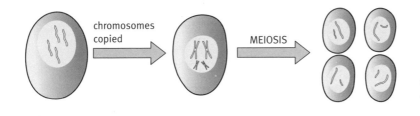

chromosomes copied

MEIOSIS

Meiosis of a cell with 4 chromosomes.

Fertilization

When a human sperm cell fertilizes an egg cell, their nuclei join up. The fertilized egg cell (**zygote**) gets one set of chromosomes from each parent. It has 23 chromosome pairs – 46 chromosomes in all.

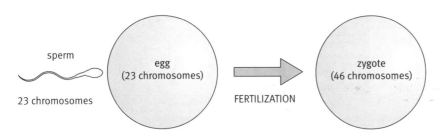

sperm

23 chromosomes

egg (23 chromosomes)

FERTILIZATION

zygote (46 chromosomes)

How genes control cell growth and development

DNA and the genetic code

The nucleus of each of your body cells contains enough information to determine the characteristics of your whole body. This information is the **genetic code**.

The genetic code is stored in chromosomes. A chromosome is a very long molecule of **DNA**. A human DNA molecule is made up of about 30 000 genes. Each gene probably contains all the information needed to make a certain protein.

A DNA molecule contains two strands twisted together in a spiral. This is a **double helix**.

▶ Each strand is made of four bases: adenine (A), thymine (T), guanine (G) and cytosine (C).

▶ The bases on the two strands of a DNA molecule always pair up in the same way: A pairs with T and G pairs with C. This is **base pairing**.

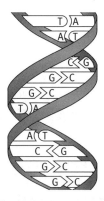

Copying DNA

When a cell grows, it makes copies of its chromosomes. Base pairing in DNA means that the copies are exact. The copies are made like this:

▶ Bonds between the bases split. So the two strands separate.
▶ The cell contains free bases. These start to make new strands.
▶ G always pairs with C, and A always pairs with T.
  So the two new strands are identical to the original strands.

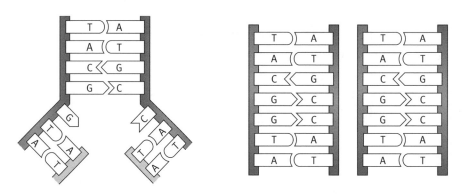

One DNA strand...   ...makes...   ...two new DNA strands

64 combinations!

nucleus
chromosome
gene
DNA
Bases

Making proteins

Cells make proteins from about 20 **amino acids**. There are thousands of different proteins. Each protein has a certain combination of amino acids joined together in a particular order.

H The order of bases in a gene is the code for joining amino acids in the correct order to make a particular protein. Each amino acid has a three-base code (a **triplet code**). So four bases can code for all 20 amino acids.

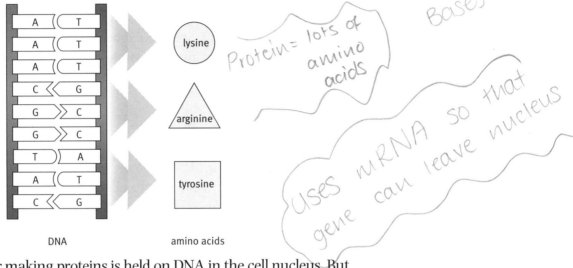

Protein = lots of amino acids

DNA   amino acids

uses mRNA so that gene can leave nucleus

The genetic code for making proteins is held on DNA in the cell nucleus. But proteins are made in ribosomes in the cell cytoplasm. Genes cannot leave the nucleus. So messenger RNA (**mRNA**) molecules transfer the genetic code from the nucleus to ribosomes. mRNA molecules are smaller than DNA, so they can fit through gaps in the membrane round the nucleus.

H mRNA differs from DNA in that it has just one strand and the base U replaces base T in DNA.

DNA = A + T
MRNA = A + U

This is how a protein is made:

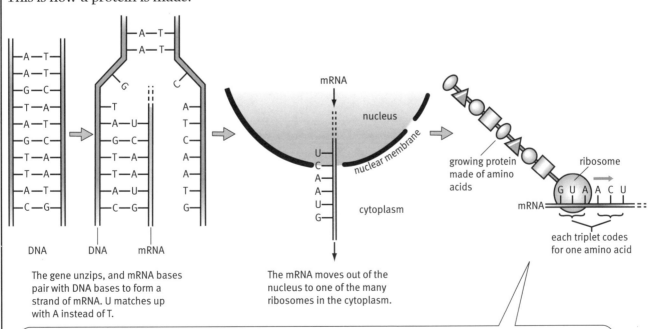

DNA   DNA   mRNA

The gene unzips, and mRNA bases pair with DNA bases to form a strand of mRNA. U matches up with A instead of T.

The mRNA moves out of the nucleus to one of the many ribosomes in the cytoplasm.

mRNA

nucleus

nuclear membrane

cytoplasm

growing protein made of amino acids

ribosome

mRNA

each triplet codes for one amino acid

The ribosome attaches to one end of the mRNA. As it moves along the mRNA, the ribosome reads the genetic code so that it can join the amino acids together in the correct order. When it has finished, the ribosome releases the protein into the cytoplasm and starts to make another one.

From single cell to whole organism

16 cell stage = specialized

Embryo development

A fertilized egg cell (zygote) divides by mitosis to make an embryo.

Up to the eight-cell stage of a human embryo, every cell is identical. Each cell can develop into any sort of cell that the organism needs – or even a whole organism. These are **embryonic stem cells**.

After the eight-cell stage, the embryo's cells become specialized. They have a particular structure to do a particular job. Specialized cells of the same type group together to form **tissues**. For example, muscle cells group together to make muscle tissue.

Gene switching

The nucleus of each of your body cells contains an exact copy of the DNA of the original zygote. So every cell contains the same genes – about 30 000 of them. But not all these genes are active in every cell. Each cell makes only the proteins it needs to be a particular type of cell. So genes that give instructions to make other proteins are not active; they are **switched off**.

For example, hair cells make keratin. So the genes for the enzymes that make keratin are switched on. Hair cells do not make muscle. So the genes for the enzymes that make muscle are switched off.

Salivary gland cells make amylase. So the genes for the enzymes that make amylase are switched on. The genes for the enzymes that make keratin and muscle are switched off.

All cells respire, so the genes needed for respiration are switched on in all cells.

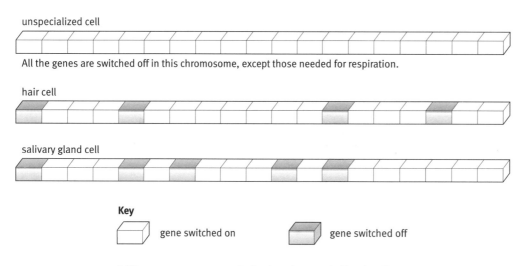

Different genes are switched on in specialized cells.

H Stem cell technology

Stem cells are unspecialized cells. They can divide and develop into specialized cells. Stem cells come from early embryos, umbilical cord blood, and adults.

Scientists hope to use stem cells to treat diseases and replace damaged tissues. For example, skin cells grown from stem cells could be used to treat burns. Nerve cells grown from stem cells could treat spinal injuries.

There are problems with stem cell technology.

▸ Embryonic stem cells are most useful, as all their genes are still switched on. But . . .
  – some people have ethical objections to using them
  – tissues grown from embryonic stem cells have different genes to the patients receiving the tissue. So patients must take drugs to stop their bodies rejecting the transplanted tissue.

▸ Adult stem cells have most of their genes switched off. So they can grow into only a few cell types.

Therapeutic cloning switches on inactive genes in adult body cell nuclei. It also overcomes the problem of patients rejecting transplanted tissue.

This is how to produce an organ or tissue needed by a patient:

▸ Take a nucleus out of a human egg cell. Replace it with a nucleus from a body cell of the patient.

▸ The egg cell makes an embryo. Its genes are the same as the patient's genes.

▸ After 5 days, put stem cells from the embryo in a dish of nutrients.

▸ The stem cells can develop into different organs and tissues.

▸ Transplant the organ or tissue required into the patient.

embryonic stem cells = unspecialized

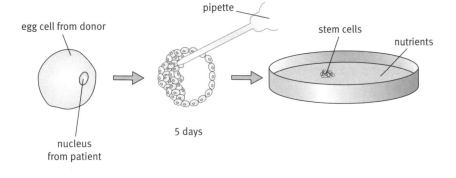

egg cell from donor

nucleus from patient

pipette

5 days

stem cells

nutrients

How plants grow and develop

Cells, tissues, and organs

Most plant cells are specialized. They group together in tissues. Groups of tissues organize themselves into organs, for example leaves, flowers, and roots.

Some plant cells remain unspecialized. These **meristem cells** can develop into any type of specialized plant cell. So plants can regrow whole organs if they are damaged.

Growth

unspecialized

Most plants grow throughout their lives. They grow when meristem cells divide to make new cells.

▶ Meristem cells in shoot tips divide to make stems taller.
▶ Meristem cells in root tips divide to make roots longer.
▶ Rings of meristem cells in stems and roots divide to make them wider.

Plants tend to grow towards the light. This is **phototropism**. Plants need light to photosynthesize. So phototropism increases a plant's chance of survival.

Phototropism involves plant hormones called **auxins**.

H

If light is above a growing shoot, auxins spread out evenly. The shoot grows straight up.

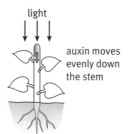

light

auxin moves evenly down the stem

If light comes from the side, auxins move to the shady side. Auxins make cells on the shady side grow faster. So the shoot bends towards the light.

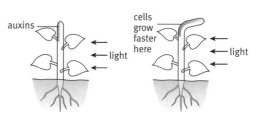

auxins

light

cells grow faster here

light

Cuttings

Gardeners sometimes grow plants that are genetically identical to a parent plant. They do this by taking **cuttings**. The new plant and the parent plant are **clones**.

First, the gardener chooses a plant with features that he wants. Then he cuts a shoot or leaf from the plant. This is a cutting. The gardener puts the cutting in water, compost or **rooting powder**. Rooting powder contains auxins.

The shoot's meristem cells divide to make new cells. Auxins encourage some of these cells to develop into root cells. Other unspecialized cells become

▶ other organs, for example flower or leaves
▶ tissues, for example xylem, which transports water, and phloem, which transports sugar.

1 Giraffes have 30 chromosomes in each body cell.

a Finish the sentences by choosing the best words and numbers from the box.

Use each word or number once, more than once, or not at all.

gametes	zygotes	different	ovaries	testes
penis	identical	1 2 4	15	30 60

Giraffes make sex cells by meiosis. Sex cells are also called

gametes. In male giraffes, meiosis happens in the

testes. In meiosis, one body cell divides to make _4_ sex

cells. Each of these cells carries _different_ genetic information.

There are _15_ chromosomes in one giraffe sex cell.   [5]

b After sexual intercourse, the nucleus of a male sex cell joins to the nucleus of a female sex cell.

i Give the name of the female sex cell.

egg   [1]

ii Give the name of the process in which the nucleus of a male sex cell joins to the nucleus of a female sex cell.

fertilisation   [1]

c The steps below describe how body cells grow and divide in giraffe embryos.
They are in the wrong order.

A The chromosome copies separate and go to opposite ends of the cell.

B These are identical to each other and to the parent cell.

C The cell makes copies of its specialised parts, including the chromosomes.

D The cell divides to make two new cells.

Fill in the boxes to show the correct order.   [3]

C A D B

Total [10]

2 James has a rose plant.

He cuts a piece of stem from the plant. This is a cutting.

He puts the cutting in rooting powder.

The cutting grows roots.

A new rose plant grows.

a i Why do gardeners take cuttings?

Tick the **two best** reasons.

They can grow many new plants quickly and cheaply. ☑

They can grow many new plants with different features by taking cuttings from just one plant. ☑✗

Plants grown from cuttings are more resistant to disease than plants grown from seed. ☐

They can reproduce a plant with exactly the features they want. ☐ ✓

Plants grown from cuttings are stronger than plants grown from seed. ☐ [1]

ii Give the name of the plant hormone in rooting powder.

Auxin [1]

iii Name the unspecialized plant cells that divide to make root cells in cuttings.

Stem cells ✗ Meristem cells [1]

iv Name two other plant organs (not roots) that are made by the division of unspecialized plant cells in cuttings.

leaves

stem [2]

b The shoot of the rose plant grows towards the light.

i Explain how growing towards the light helps the plant to survive.

Recieving more light means photosynthesis happens.

[1]

ii Give the scientific name for the process in which growing plant shoots bend towards the light.

Phototropism

[1]

H

iii The drawing shows the shoot of a rose plant.
The arrows show the direction of the light.

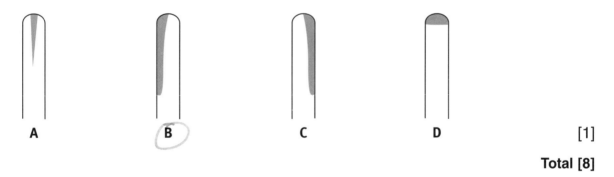

In which drawing below does the shaded area show where the concentration of plant hormones is greatest?

Draw a (ring) around the correct answer.

A   B   C   D   [1]

Total [8]

3 A company sells 'stem cell gift certificates'.

When a baby is born, a nurse takes blood from the baby's umbilical cord. The company separates stem cells from the blood. It stores the stem cells at −180 °C for 25 years.

a i What are stem cells?

Put a tick next to the **best** definition.

Stem cells are unspecialized cells. They join together to make specialized cells. ☑

Stem cells are unspecialized cells. They divide and develop into specialized cells. ☑

Stem cells are specialized cells. They divide and develop into unspecialized cells. ☐

Stem cells are specialized cells. They join together to make unspecialized cells. ☐ [1]

ii The company says that doctors can use the stem cells to treat illnesses the baby may get in future.

How might doctors use the stem cells to treat heart disease?

Put a tick next to the **most likely** answer.

They will make a heart disease vaccine from the stem cells. ☐

They will grow heart muscle cells from the stem cells. ☑

They will make a heart disease medicine from the stem cells. ☑

They will inject stem cells into the patient's bloodstream. ☐ [1]

b One source of stem cells is umbilical cord blood.

i Name **one other** source of stem cells.

embryo [1]

ii Give one **problem** of using stem cells from this source to treat disease or replace damaged tissues.

body may reject it

[1]

iii Read this leaflet. It is written by people who think that umbilical cord stem cells should not be taken and stored.

Warning to women about to give birth

Do you have a stem cell gift certificate? We suggest you don't use it.

Scientists hope umbilical cord stem cells will cure many diseases in future. But so far these stem cells have cured only very few diseases. It is unlikely that your child will get one of these diseases.

Taking blood from the umbilical cord is not easy. It will distract midwives when they should be concentrating on making sure that the mother and baby are safe and well.

We also don't know how long stem cells can be stored for.

Why might doctors give pregnant women this warning?

Put a tick next to the **three best** answers.

Taking blood from the umbilical cord could harm the mother or baby.	✓
Umbilical cord stem cells can produce red blood cells only.	☐
So far, there has only been little success in using stem cells to treat disease.	✓
There is only a small risk of getting diseases that stem cells could treat.	✓
Umbilical cord stem cells can produce white blood cells only.	☐

[3]

Total [7]

4 a The picture shows part of a DNA molecule.

A DNA molecule contains two strands twisted together in a spiral.

Give the name of the structure.

___Double Helix_____ [1]

H **b** Human DNA molecules contain up to 30 000 genes.

What does a gene do?

Tick the correct answer.

It gives instructions for joining amino acids in the correct order to make a certain base. ☐

It gives instructions for joining bases in the correct order to make a certain amino acid. ☑

It gives instructions for joining bases in the correct order to make a certain protein. ☐

It gives instructions for joining amino acids in the correct order to make a certain protein. ☐ [1]

c The steps below describe how a DNA molecule makes an exact copy of itself.

They are in the wrong order.

A The DNA molecule opens up from one end and makes two single strands.

B Bonds between base pairs break.

C The free bases join together to make two new strands.

D Free bases in the cell line up next to the single strands.

Fill in the boxes to show the correct order.

| B | A | D | C |

[3]

Total [5]

1 Match each word with its definition.

Word	Definition
behaviour	A change in the environment
stimulus	An action caused by a change in the environment
response	Anything an animal does

2 Each picture shows one newborn reflex.

Add a caption to each picture that **names and describes** the reflex.

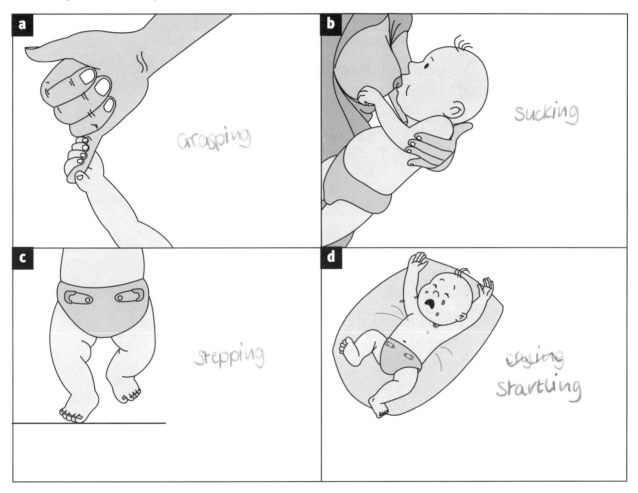

a Grasping

b sucking

c stepping

d crying Startling

3 Write **S** next to the sentences that best apply to simple animals, like woodlice.

Write **C** next to the sentences that best apply to complex animals, like horses.

a These animals rely on reflex actions for most of their behaviour. S

b These animals can change their behaviour. S C

c These animals find it difficult to respond to new situations. C S

d These animals are less likely to survive environmental changes. S

e These animals can learn to link a new stimulus to a reflex action. C

4 Write the letters of the receptors and effectors below in the correct column of the table.

A Skin cells that detect pain

B Cells in your retina that detect light

C Muscle cells in a baby's fingers that make him grip your finger tightly

D A sweat gland that releases sweat when you are nervous

E Taste buds on your tongue

F The semi-circular canals in your ears that detect movement

G The salivary gland that releases saliva when you smell food

H Muscle cells in your quadriceps that contract when someone hits you below the knee

Receptors	Effectors
A F B E	C D H G

5 The diagram shows a reflex arc.

Use these words to label the diagram.

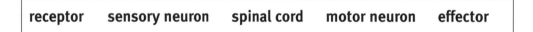

| receptor | sensory neuron | spinal cord | motor neuron | effector |

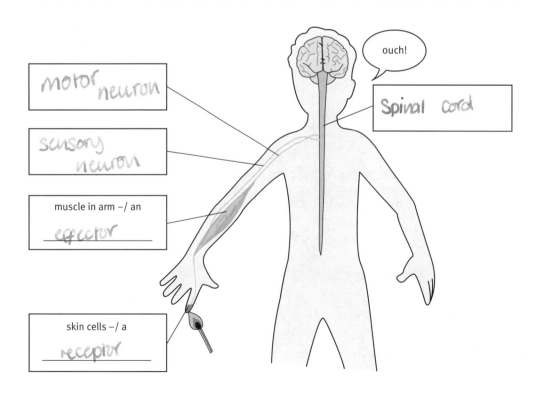

motor neuron

sensory neuron

muscle in arm –/ an

effector

skin cells –/ a

receptor

ouch!

Spinal cord

6 The stages below describe how information is passed along a simple reflex arc. They are in the wrong order.

   A A receptor cell detects dust in your eye.

   B The effectors (muscles in your eyelid) blink to remove the dust.

   C The CNS receives the impulses.

   D The CNS processes the information.

   E The CNS sends an electrical impulse along a motor neuron to the effectors.

   F A sensory neuron carries electrical impulses to your central nervous system (CNS).

Fill in the boxes to show the correct order. The first one has been done for you.

| A | F | C | D | E | B |

7 The diagram shows a motor neuron.

Complete the labels to describe what each part of the cell does.

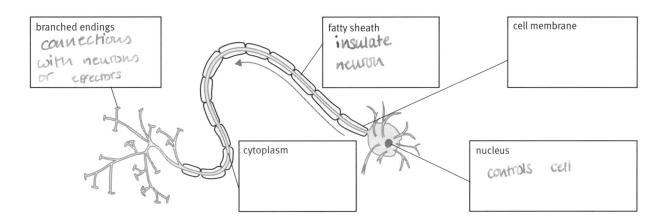

branched endings
connections with neurons or effectors

fatty sheath
insulate neuron

cell membrane

cytoplasm

nucleus
controls cell

H 8 The cartoon shows the benefits of one conditioned reflex action.

Complete the thought bubbles to describe the benefits.

1   *Mmm... that red and yellow caterpillar looks delicious!*

2   *Good. She's learnt that lesson. It'll help her to survive because...*

Yuk! That's foul! It tastes revolting!

Excellent. That'll help me survive because...

H **9** The diagrams show how a nerve impulse crosses a synapse.
They are in the wrong order.

  ▶ Number each box to show the correct sequence.

  ▶ Write notes next to each diagram to explain the process.

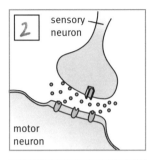

_____

_____

_____

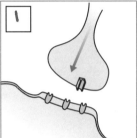

_____

_____

_____

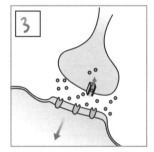

_____

_____

_____

10 The statements below are about memory.

Write the letter for each statement in
the correct part of the Venn diagram.

  A This lasts about 30 seconds.

  B This can last a lifetime.

  C There is a limit to how much we can
      remember here.

  D There is no limit to how much we can
      remember here.

  E This is the storage and retrieval of information
      by the brain.

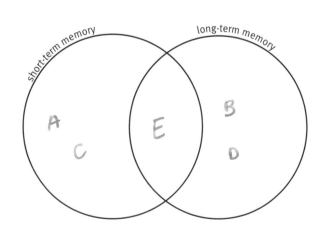

11 The diagram shows the human brain.

Complete the sentences.

a Your cerebral cortex is concerned with

C <u>onsciousness</u>

L <u>anguage</u>

I <u>ntelligence</u>

M <u>emory</u>

b Different areas of the cortex have different jobs.

Scientists have mapped these areas by <u>a multistore</u>

<u>model</u>.

c You have many potential pathways in your brain so you can

<u>learn many new things</u>

<u> </u>.

d Your brain has billions of n <u>eurons</u>.

They are connected together in complicated p <u>athways</u>.

12 The stages below describe how new pathways develop in your brain when you learn to ice skate.

They are in the wrong order.

A You ice skate for the first time.

B More impulses go along the same pathway.

C There is now a new connection between the neurons.

D Nerve impulses travel along the pathway more easily.

E You go ice skating again.

F A nerve travels along a certain pathway, from one neuron to another, for the first time.

G The connection between the neurons gets stronger.

H You now find it much easier to ice skate.

Fill in the boxes to show the correct order.

The first one has been done for you.

| A | F | C | E | B | D | G | H |

13 Solve the clues to fill in the arrow word.

1↓ S	S	2↓ S	E	N	S	U	O	I	C	S	N	O	3← ↓ C
E		Y	4↓	5→									E
R		N											6← R
O		A	7→				8→						E
T		P	9→ F	E	R	E	L				10←		B
O		S	11→	L	A	R	B	E	R	E	12← C		R
N		E	13→								14←		A
I	↑							16→					L
17→ N	15→												

Horizontal

3 Being aware of yourself and your surroundings.

5 An explanation for how human memory works.

6 Going over something again and again helps you to learn by _____.

7 A place where you can buy things!

8 The biceps _____ in your right arm is an effector.

9 _____ children do not learn to speak.

10 A long, thin extension of the cytoplasm of a neuron.

11 The brain and spinal cord form the _____.

12 This part of the brain is concerned with consciousness, memory, language, and intelligence.

13 The symbol for nitrogen.

14 In the brain, neurons are connected in _____.

15 This sort of memory lasts about 30 seconds.

16 No _____ of memory gives a full explanation of how memory works.

17 A _____ studies how the brain works.

Vertical

1 Some brain synapses release this chemical. It gives a feeling of pleasure.

2 A tiny gap between neurons.

3 The _____ cortex is concerned with memory, intelligence, consciousness, and learning.

4 A nerve cell.

15 A change in the environment that causes a response.

Responding to changes in the environment

You are at a party. As more people arrive, the room gets hotter. You start to sweat more.

A change in your environment, or **stimulus** (the increase in temperature), has triggered a **response** (increased sweating). Sweating is an example of **behaviour**. Behaviour is an animal's response to stimuli; it is everything an animal does.

Animals respond to stimuli to keep themselves in conditions that help them survive.

Simple reflex actions

If you walk into a dark room, your pupils immediately get bigger. This is a **simple reflex action**. Reflexes are automatic, or **involuntary**. They happen very quickly.

Simple reflexes make animals respond to stimuli in ways that help them survive. They help animals to

 ▸ find food
 ▸ find a mate
 ▸ escape or shelter from predators

Simple animals rely on reflex actions for most of their behaviour. So they always respond in the same way to a particular stimulus. For example, woodlice move away from light.

It is difficult for simple animals to respond to new situations. So they often fail to survive environmental changes.

A human baby shows **newborn reflexes**, including

 ▸ **grasping** – tightly gripping a finger in their palm
 ▸ **sucking** a nipple or finger in their mouth
 ▸ **stepping** when their feet touch a flat surface
 ▸ **startling** – spreading out arms and legs when they hear a loud noise

Babies gradually replace these reflexes with behaviours learned from experience.

The **pupil reflex** stops bright light damaging sensitive cells in the retina.

Simple animals always respond to a stimulus in the same way. These woodlice are moving away from the light.

 ▸ In bright light, muscles in the iris contract. The pupil gets smaller, so less light enters the eye.

 ▸ In dim light, different muscles in the iris contract. The pupil gets bigger, so more light enters the eye.

☐ Conditioned reflex actions

Complex animals can learn to link a new stimulus to a reflex action. So they can change their behaviour.

For example, Pavlov taught a dog to salivate when it heard a bell ring:

▶ The dog's simple reflex was to salivate when it was given food.
▶ Pavlov rang a bell while the dog was eating.
▶ After a while, the dog salivated every time it heard the bell – even if there was no food!

The stimulus (hearing the bell) became linked to food. The stimulus led to the reflex action of salivating. The final response had no direct connection to the stimulus. This is a **conditioned reflex action**.

Conditioned reflexes increase an animal's chance of survival. For example, many bitter-tasting caterpillars are brightly coloured. When a bird tastes these caterpillars, it learns not to eat them. If the caterpillar is poisonous, this conditioned reflex makes the bird more likely to survive, too.

1.) Receptor
2.) Sensory neuron
3.) Motor neuron
4.) Effector

The nervous system

The reflex arc

In a simple reflex, nerve cells carry **nerve impulses** from one part of the **nervous system** to the next. This pathway is the **reflex arc**.

▶ A **receptor** cell detects a stimulus.

▶ A **sensory neuron** carries nerve impulses as electrical signals to the **central nervous system** (**CNS**).

▶ The CNS is the brain and spinal cord. It coordinates responses to stimuli.

▶ A **motor neuron** carries nerve impulses as electrical signals from the CNS to an **effector**.

▶ The effector takes action in response to the stimulus.

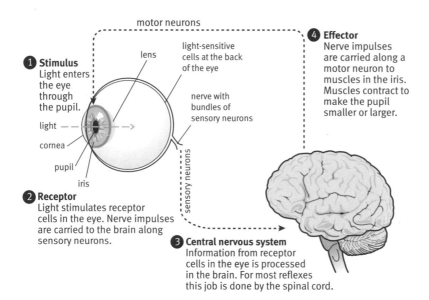

motor neurons

❶ Stimulus
Light enters the eye through the pupil.

lens

light-sensitive cells at the back of the eye

nerve with bundles of sensory neurons

light

cornea

pupil

iris

sensory neurons

❷ Receptor
Light stimulates receptor cells in the eye. Nerve impulses are carried to the brain along sensory neurons.

❹ Effector
Nerve impulses are carried along a motor neuron to muscles in the iris. Muscles contract to make the pupil smaller or larger.

❸ Central nervous system
Information from receptor cells in the eye is processed in the brain. For most reflexes this job is done by the spinal cord.

An example of a reflex arc

The peripheral nervous system

The sensory and motor neurons of the **peripheral nervous system** link the CNS to the rest of the body.

↳ everything, but not brain or spine

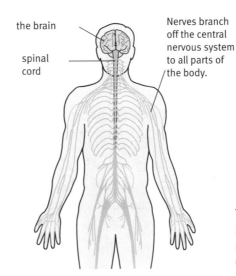

the brain

spinal cord

Nerves branch off the central nervous system to all parts of the body.

The peripheral nervous system links the brain and spinal cord with the rest of the body.

Receptors

Receptors include:

▶ single cells, such as pain sensor cells in the skin
▶ cells in complex organs, such as **light-sensitive cells** in the retina. These detect light and send nerve impulses along neurons to the brain.

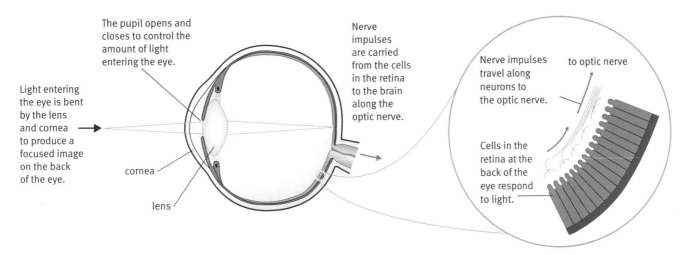

The pupil opens and closes to control the amount of light entering the eye.

Nerve impulses are carried from the cells in the retina to the brain along the optic nerve.

Nerve impulses travel along neurons to the optic nerve.

to optic nerve

Light entering the eye is bent by the lens and cornea to produce a focused image on the back of the eye.

cornea

lens

Cells in the retina at the back of the eye respond to light.

Light is focused by the cornea and lens onto light-sensitive cells at the back of the eye. These cells are receptors. They trigger nerve impulses to the brain.

Effectors

Effectors are either **muscles** or **glands.** When they are stimulated by nerve impulses:

▶ muscle cells contract to move a part of the body – for example, you 'gag' when something touches the back of your throat

▶ glands release chemicals, for example sweat or hormones

Neurons

Nerves are bundles of specialized cells called **neurons**. Neurons have a nucleus, cytoplasm, and a cell membrane.

▶ The nucleus is in the **cell body**.
▶ The cytoplasm is a long, thin fibre. It is surrounded by the cell membrane. This is the **axon**.

Some axons are surrounded by a **fatty sheath**. The fatty sheath insulates the neuron from neighbouring cells. This means that electrical nerve impulses can travel along the neuron very quickly.

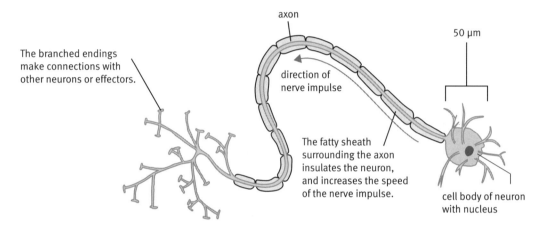

axon

50 μm

The branched endings make connections with other neurons or effectors.

direction of nerve impulse

The fatty sheath surrounding the axon insulates the neuron, and increases the speed of the nerve impulse.

cell body of neuron with nucleus

A motor neuron

Synapses

Synapses are tiny gaps between neurons. Nerve impulses must cross these gaps when they travel from one neuron to the next.

H Chemicals pass an impulse across the synapse from one neuron to the next.

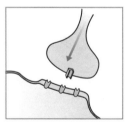

1 A nerve impulse gets to the end of a sensory neuron.

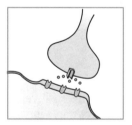

2 The sensory neuron releases a chemical into the synapse.

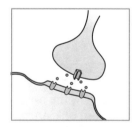

3 The chemical diffuses across the synapse.

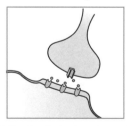

4 The chemical arrives at receptor molecules on the motor neuron's membrane. The chemical's molecules are the correct shape to bind to the receptor molecules.

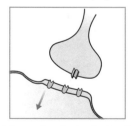

5 A nerve impulse is stimulated in the motor neuron.

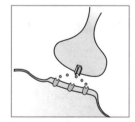

6 The chemical is absorbed back into the sensory neuron to be used again.

Some drugs and poisons affect the transmission of nerve impulses across synapses.

H The chemical **serotonin** is released at some synapses in the brain. This gives a feeling of pleasure. Sensory neurons later remove the serotonin. This is a natural process.

The drug **Ecstasy** (MDMA) blocks the places that remove serotonin. So the serotonin concentration in the synapse increases. This can make Ecstasy users feel happy for a while. But Ecstasy is very harmful. It interferes with temperature control systems and can kill. Long-term users suffer anxiety and depression.

blocks receptor molecules.

Consciously controlling reflexes

Sometimes the brain consciously changes a reflex response. For example:

▶ You pick up a hot plate of delicious food. A nerve impulse travels along a sensory neuron to your spinal cord. Your reflex response is to drop the plate.

▶ But another nerve impulse travels up your spine to your brain. It comes back down to the motor neuron and makes a muscle movement in your arm that stops the reflex response.

▶ You keep hold of the plate until you can put it down safely.

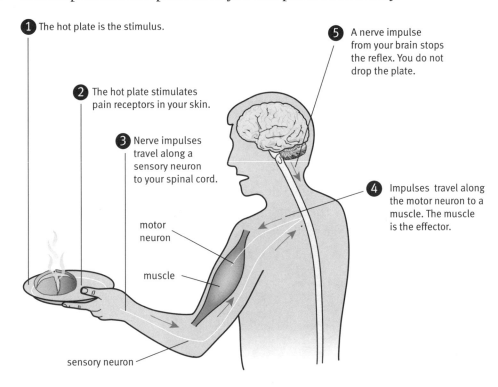

1 The hot plate is the stimulus.

2 The hot plate stimulates pain receptors in your skin.

3 Nerve impulses travel along a sensory neuron to your spinal cord.

motor neuron

muscle

sensory neuron

5 A nerve impulse from your brain stops the reflex. You do not drop the plate.

4 Impulses travel along the motor neuron to a muscle. The muscle is the effector.

Developing complex behaviour

Mammals – including humans – can change their behaviour as a result of new experiences. This is **learning**.

Mammals have complex brains with billions of neurons. The neurons are connected together in complicated **pathways**. Learning new things creates new pathways. There are many potential pathways in the brain. So animals can adapt to new situations and learn to interact effectively with others.

New pathways develop as a result of practice and repetition.

▶ You experience something new.

▶ A nerve impulse travels along a particular pathway, from one neuron to another, for the first time. There are new connections between the neurons.

▶ You repeat the experience.

▶ More impulses go along the same pathway. The connections between the neurons get stronger.

▶ Nerve impulses travel along the pathway more easily. It is easier to respond in the way that you practised.

As the drummer practises, he strengthens pathways between certain neurons in his brain. So he gets better and better!

H Children can only acquire some skills at a certain age. For example, a **feral** (wild) child cannot learn to speak if found after the time in development when they would normally have learnt language skills.

The cortex
Mapping the cortex
Different regions of the brain's cortex have different jobs. Neuroscientists map the cortex by:

▶ studying patients with brain damage

▶ electrically stimulating different parts of the brain

▶ doing MRI scans of the brain – these show which parts of the brain are most active when a person does different things

Memory
Intelligence
Language
Consciousness

The **cerebral cortex** is the region most concerned with **intelligence**, language, memory, and **consciousness** (being aware of yourself and your surroundings).

Memory

Memory is the storage and retrieval of information by the brain. Verbal **memory** is stored information about words and language.

There are two types of verbal memory. They work separately in the brain.

▶ **Short-term memory** lasts about 30 seconds.

▶ **Long-term memory** is a seemingly limitless store of information that can last a lifetime.

Psychologists have devised various models to explain how memory works. One of these is called the **multistore** model. However, no model gives a full explanation.

Humans use different ways to help them remember information:

▶ Looking for patterns, or organizing information to make a pattern. If you can see a pattern, you process the information more deeply.

For example, Dan's shopping list is organized into groups. Jordan's list isn't. Most people would find it easier to remember Dan's shopping list.

Dan's list   **Jordan's list**

▶ Repeating the information as much as possible. For example, actors learn their lines by going over them again and again and again.

▶ Associating the information with a strong stimulus, for example light, colour, a smell, or music. So a whiff of perfume might remind you of a friend who wears that perfume, or a piece of music might bring back happy or sad memories.

1 This question is about reflex actions.

   a Sarah is five months old. Look at the list of things that she does.

     Tick the **two** actions that are newborn reflexes.

     She grips a finger that is put into the palm of her hand. ☑

     She stops crying when her sister sings to her. ☐

     She spreads out her arms and legs when she hears a sudden noise. ☑

     She cries when her favourite toy is taken away. ☐

     She goes to sleep in her pram. ☐ [2]

   b Until she was two months old, Sarah sucked anything that was put into her mouth.

     Complete the sentences.

     Sucking is the response to the stimulus of _something put into her mouth_.

     The newborn sucking reflex helped Sarah's survival by making sure she got enough _food/milk_. [2]

   c Humans rely on reflex actions for only some of their behaviour.

     Worms rely on reflex actions for most of their behaviour.

     Give one disadvantage of relying on simple reflex actions for most behaviour.

     can't respond to new situations

     [1]

     Total [5]

2 a Draw a line to match each part of the nervous system to its job.

Part of nervous system	Job
effector cells	control the body's response to a stimulus
receptor cells	detect a stimulus
brain and spinal cord	make changes in response to a stimulus

[2]

b Josh is crossing the road. He sees a car coming towards him.

A nerve signal travels from his eyes to his adrenal glands.

His adrenal glands release a hormone, adrenaline.

The adrenaline helps Josh to get out of the way of the car before it hits him.

i The path taken by the nerve signal is shown in the diagram.

Use these words to finish labelling the diagram.

sensory neuron	motor neuron	central nervous system

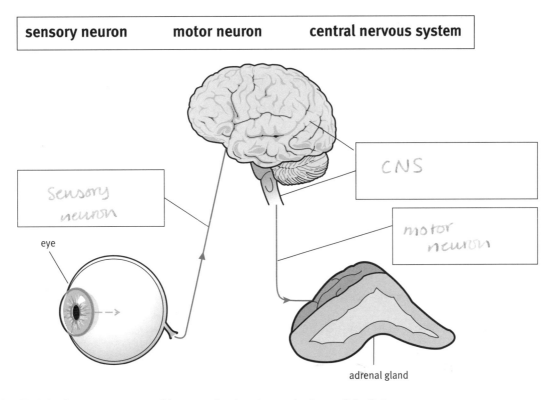

Sensory neuron

eye

CNS

motor neuron

adrenal gland

[3]

ii Finish the sentences. Choose the best words from this list.

Use each word once, more than once or not at all.

peripheral	central	electrical	chemical

The signal is carried along nerve cells by _electrical_ impulses.

The sensory and motor neurons are part of the _peripheral_ nervous

system. The brain and spinal cord form the _central_ nervous system. [3]

Total [8]

3 Dolphins are mammals.

    a Dolphins can adapt to new situations.

       Tick the statement that **best** explains why.

        Dolphins have billions of neurons. ☐

        A dolphin's brain has a great variety of potential neuron pathways. ☑

        Dolphins respond to stimuli by both simple and conditioned reflex actions. ☐

        Dolphins can learn reflex responses to new stimuli. ☑

        The average dolphin's brain has a mass of 1.6 kg. ☐   [1]

    b The steps below describe how a dolphin learns to jump through a hoop.

       They are in the wrong order.

       A The dolphin jumps through a hoop for the first time.

       B More nerve impulses travel along the same pathway.

       C A nerve impulse travels along a pathway between two neurons in the brain for the first time.

       D The dolphin jumps through the hoop again.

       E This makes a connection between the two neurons.

       F This makes the connection between the two neurons stronger.

       G It is now easier for nerve impulses to travel along the pathway, and so easier for the dolphin to jump through hoops.

       Fill in the boxes to show the correct order.

       The first and last ones have been done for you.

        A   C   E   D   B   F   G   [4]

                                                      Total [5]

H **4** **a** Louise has a cat called Tibbles.

When Tibbles hears Louise use a tin-opener, he produces saliva.

Finish the sentences. Choose the best words from this list.

Use each word once, more than once or not at all.

response	learned	conditioned	simple	stimulus

The sound of Louise using a tin-opener is the ___stimulus___ .

Tibbles production of saliva is the ___response___ . The response

has no direct connection to the stimulus. Tibbles has ___learned___

the response. So this is a ___conditioned___ reflex action.   [4]

b Wasps are insects. They are black and yellow.

   i A bird has learned that wasps taste bitter.

   The bird never eats black and yellow insects.

   Explain how this behaviour might help the bird survive.

   It has learnt that black + yellow are
   nasty tasting so it won't eat it
   again.   [1]

   ii Hover flies are also black and yellow.

   They do not have a bitter taste.

   Explain how the hover fly's colouring helps it to survive.

   The colours are associated with a
   bitter tasting insect.   [1]

Total [6]

5 Synapses are gaps between neighbouring neurons.

a The statements describe how nerve impulses cross a synapse.

They are in the wrong order.

A A nerve impulse arrives at the synapse.

B Molecules of the chemical fit into receptor molecules on the motor neuron.

C A chemical is released from the sensory neuron.

D The chemical is absorbed back into the sensory neuron to be used again.

E The chemical diffuses across the synapse.

F A nerve impulse is stimulated in the motor neuron.

Fill in the boxes to show the correct order.

The first one has been done for you.

| A | C | E | F | B | D |

B   F

[4]

b The drug Ecstasy affects the transmission of impulses across synapses.

Ticks the **two** statements that best explain how.

Ecstasy causes a decrease in the concentration of serotonin in the brain. ☐

Ecstasy makes it easier for synapses in the brain to remove serotonin. ☐

Ecstasy makes sensory neurons release more serotonin. ☐

Ecstasy causes an increase in the concentration of serotonin in the brain. ☑

Ecstasy blocks sites in the brain's synapses where serotonin is removed. ☑

Ecstasy makes sensory neurons release less serotonin. ☐

[2]

Total [6]

1 a Complete the diagram to show what happens to the light energy that reaches a leaf.

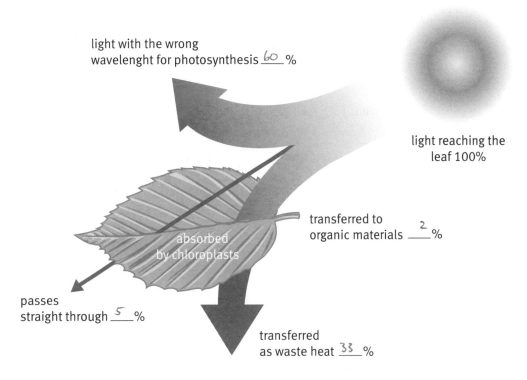

light with the wrong wavelenght for photosynthesis _60_ %

light reaching the leaf 100%

transferred to organic materials _2_%

absorbed by chloroplasts

passes straight through _5_%

transferred as waste heat _33_%

b What percentage of light reaching a leaf is absorbed by chloroplasts? _____2%_____

2 Match the terms to their definitions as shown.

autotrophs — micro-organisms that feed on and decay dead organisms

carnivores — organisms which produce their own organic compounds

decomposers — organisms that obtain organic compounds by eating other organisms

herbivores — organisms that are able to make their own food; they are the autotrophs at the start of food chains

heterotrophs — animals that feed on other animals

producers — animals that feed on plants; they are primary consumers

3 Look at the food chains.

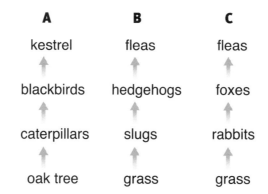

A	B	C
kestrel	fleas	fleas
↑	↑	↑
blackbirds	hedgehogs	foxes
↑	↑	↑
caterpillars	slugs	rabbits
↑	↑	↑
oak tree	grass	grass

a Which chain belongs to an ecosystem that matches each of these pyramids of numbers?

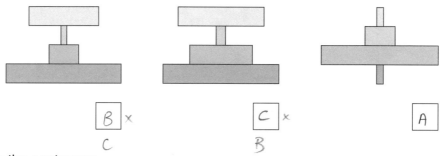

B ✗
C

C ✗
B

A

b Complete the sentences.

A pyramid of ___biomass~~numbers~~___ for an ecosystem shows the mass of the organisms at each

___trophic___ level. It shows how much ___~~energy~~ mass___ passes from one level to the next.

4 **a** Fill in the five boxes using these words.

primary consumer   producer   secondary consumer   the Sun   tertiary consumer

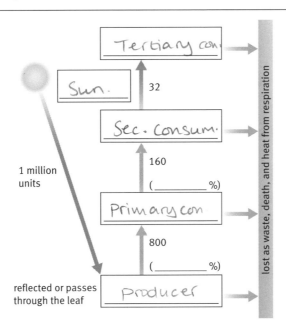

b The _producer_ in this ecosystem transformed 10 000 of 1 000 000 units of energy into biomass. 800 of these units were transferred to _primary_ consumers.

c Calculate the percentage of the energy transferred from

i producers to primary consumers $\frac{800}{10,000} \times 100 = 8\%$

ii primary consumers to secondary consumers. $\frac{160}{800} \times 100 = 20\%$

Why do we need the Sun?
The Sun provides the
 ▶ thermal energy that helps to keep the Earth's atmosphere warm
 ▶ light energy that green plants use to make food chemicals

Animals, fungi and bacteria depend, directly or indirectly on plants for food.
So life on Earth is dependent on energy from the Sun.

How do plants harness the Sun's energy?
Only the green parts of plants absorb light energy.
They use it to make food in a process called **photosynthesis**.

Plants absorb only a tiny percentage of the Sun's energy.

The new material made by photosynthesis consists of chemicals such as **carbohydrates, fats** and **proteins**. These chemicals form new plant cells and any food stores inside those cells. You can think of both as a store of energy.

Do all organisms in the ecosystem feed in the same way?
We call organisms that make their own food **autotrophs**. Most are green plants. A few non-green microorganisms are also autotrophs. They don't use light to make their food.

Organisms that can't make their own food are called **heterotrophs**. These include animals, bacteria and fungi. They depend on the food produced by autotrophs.

If heterotrophs feed on . . .	. . . we call them . . .
plants	herbivores
animals that have eaten plants	carnivores
waste produced by plants and animals	decomposers

How are food and energy transferred between organisms in an ecosystem?

When an animal eats a plant, the energy stored in the plant is transferred to the animal. The chemicals in waste material and dead plants and animals are also an energy store. The energy in these is transferred to the decomposers that feed on them.

We can show what eats what using food chains. Foods chains also show the direction of energy transfer too.

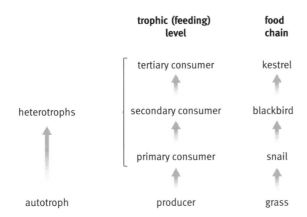

A **pyramid of numbers** shows the numbers of organisms at each feeding level in an ecosystem. It gives you no idea of the biomass at each level.

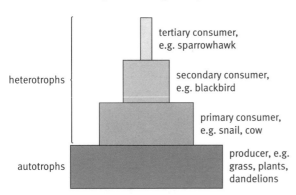

A **pyramid of biomass** shows the mass of organisms at each feeding level. So it shows how much food is available to the next level.

Pyramid of **biomass** for oak woodland

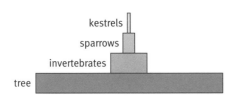

A pyramid of biomass is bigger at the base than at the top because some of the mass does not pass on to the next level.

Pyramid of **numbers** for oak woodland

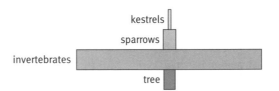

If lots of smaller organisms feed on a few large ones in an ecosystem, a pyramid of numbers isn't a pyramid shape.

How is energy lost from food chains?

There is less biomass at each level in a food chain. So there is less energy. The energy that is not passed on is:

 ▶ in uneaten parts

 ▶ that used for life processes such as movement and keeping warm

 ▶ lost to the surroundings as heat energy

 ▶ in waste products

As there is less food and energy at each feeding level, there is a limit to the length of food chains.

You need to be able to calculate the percentage efficiency of energy transfer at different stages of a food chain.

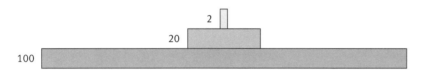

If 2 units of energy out of 20 are transferred, the percentage transferred is

$$\frac{2}{20} \times 100 = 10\%$$

What is in soil?

Soil contains:

 ▶ biomass. That includes the living organisms and decaying materials

 ▶ inorganic particles such as sand, silt and clay

 ▶ air

 ▶ water with dissolved mineral ions

To calculate the percentage of water:

$$\text{Mass of soil at the start} = 50 \text{ g}$$

$$\text{Mass of soil when dried to constant mass} = 35 \text{ g}$$

$$\text{Loss of mass (or water lost)} = 15 \text{ g}$$

$$\% \text{ loss} = \frac{15}{50} \times 100$$

$$= 30\%$$

You can calculate the percentage of biomass in a similar way after burning all the biomass in dried soil. The percentage of all the components of soil varies from time to time and place to place. So it is sensible to take the mean of several sets of results.

1 Food webs show what eats what else in a particular habitat or ecosystem.

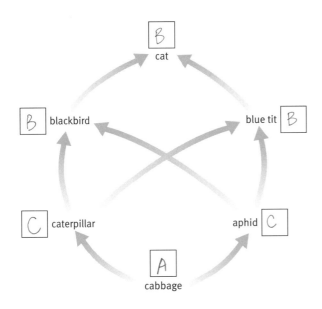

a Identify the following parts of this food web, by writing the correct letters in the boxes.

   A a producer

   B a tertiary consumer

   C an autotroph   [3]

b Write down **one** food chain from this food web.

   __Cabbage → aphid → blue tit → cat__   [1]

c Use words from the list to complete the sentences.

dead	kills	eaten	eats	heat	materials	moving	energy	warm	waste

   When one organism __kills ✗ eats.__ another, only about 10 per cent of the __energy__ is

   transferred to the organism. This is because some of the energy is transferred in life

   processes such as __moving__ and keeping __warm__, and some is transferred to the

   surroundings as __heat__. Also, some energy remains in undigested __waste__.

   In the same way, when decomposers feed on __dead__ organisms and waste

   __materials__, only part of the energy is transferred.   [8]

                                                             Total [12]

2 a What is the source of energy for food chains?

~~autotroph~~ The Sun.   [1]

b Green plants can use this energy to make food chemicals.

What term describes organisms that can make their own food? _autotroph._   [1]

c Write down **two** food chemicals that are stores of energy in cells.

Carbohydrates and _fats_   [2]

d In the box next to the biomass pyramid, draw an arrow to show the direction in which the energy passes.

sharks
herrings
zooplankton
phytoplankton

↑   [1]

e Which level of the biomass pyramid contains the least energy?

Explain why this is.

Sharks as the trophic level is the

least.   [3]

f The amount of energy in the herrings is 200 units. The amount transferred to the sharks is 28 units.

Calculate the percentage of the energy that is transferred. Show your working.

$^{28}/_{200} \times 100$

$= 14\%$ [2]

Total [10]

3 Ian and Holly counted the numbers of visible organisms at each trophic level in an aquarium.

Their results are shown in the table.

Trophic level	Number
tertiary consumers	2
secondary consumers	12
primary consumers	30
producers	95

a Using the information in the table, draw a pyramid of numbers. Use the scale 1 mm represents 1 organism. Remember to label the levels.

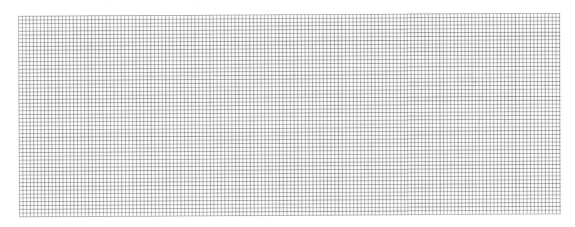

[5]

b The table below shows Ian's results for a food chain based on only one kind of plant in the aquarium.

Trophic level	Number
tertiary consumers	1
secondary consumers	2
primary consumers	7
producers	1

Draw the shape of the pyramid of numbers for these data. Label the levels.

[5]

c   Explain why the two pyramids are different.

One shows mass whereas one shows the number of organism.

[3]

d   Holly suggested that it would be better to draw pyramids of biomass for the two sets of data. Suggest why.

So that it is easier to compare.

[2]

e   In the boxes, sketch the shapes of the two pyramids of biomass. Do not add labels.   [4]

Whole aquarium

One plant

Total [19]

4 a Write down **one** component of soil missing from this list.

_____air_____ [1]

  ▶ biomass; that includes the living organisms and decaying materials

  ▶ inorganic particles such as sand, silt and clay

  ▶ water with dissolved mineral ions

b In an experiment, Alex heated a sample of soil gently to evaporate all the water. Then he heated it strongly to burn off the biomass. These are his results.

Original mass of soil sample = 25 g

Mass of dried soil = 20 g

Mass of soil after strong heating = 18 g

difference = 2g

i Calculate the percentage of the original mass of the soil that was biomass. Show your working.

$\frac{2}{25} \times 100 =$ 8%

_____

_____

ii Calculate the percentage mass of the original soil that remains at the end of the experiment. Show your working.

$\frac{18}{25} \times 100 = 72\%$

_____

_____ [4]

Total [5]

1 Complete the flowchart. Use these words.

amino acids	carbon dioxide	cellulose	chemicals	chlorophyll	fat
glucose	light energy	oxygen	protein	respiration	starch	water

Chlorophyll absorbs _light_ _energy_

↓

Atoms from _carbon_ _dioxide_ and _water_ are rearranged

Carbohydrate (_glucose_)

Waste product (_oxygen_)

Glucose is the starting point for making lots of _chemicals_ ~~cellulose~~ in cells.

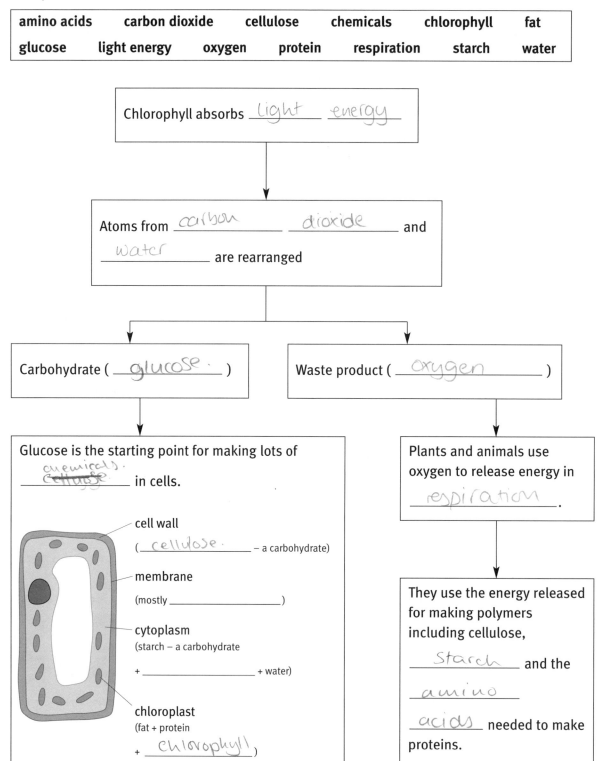

cell wall
(_cellulose_ – a carbohydrate)

membrane
(mostly _____)

cytoplasm
(starch – a carbohydrate
+ _____ + water)

chloroplast
(fat + protein
+ _chlorophyll_)

Plants and animals use oxygen to release energy in _respiration_ .

They use the energy released for making polymers including cellulose, _starch_ and the _amino_ _acids_ needed to make proteins.

2 True or false?

a Proteins are made from amino acids. __T__ ✓

b Chloroplast is a green chemical that absorbs light. __F__ ×

c Gardeners burn paraffin in greenhouses mainly to increase the amount
   of light. __F__ ✓

[H] d Plant roots absorb nitrates by active transport. __T__ ✓

e All scientists agree that human activity is causing an increase in the
   concentration of carbon dioxide in the air. __T__ × F

f Cellulose is a polymer. __F__ × T

[H] g Starch is soluble so it is a better storage molecule than glucose. __F__ ✓

What happens during photosynthesis?

The equation for photosynthesis shows only the reactants and the end products.

$$6CO_2 + 6H_2O \xrightarrow[\text{chlorophyll}]{\text{light energy}} C_6H_{12}O_6 + 6O_2$$

carbon dioxide   water   glucose   oxygen

- The green chemical chlorophyll absorbs light.
- The energy is used to rearrange the atoms of carbon dioxide and water.
- The products are glucose (a sugar) and oxygen (a waste product).

How do plants use the glucose?

Plants

- convert some of the glucose into chemicals needed for growth of plant cells, such as cellulose, protein and chlorophyll
- convert some into starch for storage
- use some in respiration to release energy.

H Because it is insoluble, starch has little effect on the osmotic balance of cells. A high concentration of glucose causes water to be drawn into cells. So, starch is a better storage molecule than glucose.

Energy released in respiration is used to synthesise polymers such as

- starch and cellulose from glucose
- amino acids and then proteins from glucose and nitrates

H Plant roots absorb nitrates by active transport, a process that requires energy.

Why does the rate of photosynthesis vary?

The rate of photosynthesis may be limited by low:

- temperatures
- carbon dioxide concentration
- light intensity.

H The amounts of carbon dioxide and oxygen exchanged over a 24-hour period vary. At compensation points, the rate of photosynthesis and respiration balance, so there is no net movement of these gases between a plant and the surrounding atmosphere

The rate of photosynthesis is limited by the factor that is in shortest supply.

1 Five students were doing a trial run for an investigation into the effect of light intensity on the rate of photosynthesis.

  ▶ They all used the same light intensity

  ▶ They measured the rate of photosynthesis by counting the bubbles of oxygen produced over a 10-minute period

  ▶ They used pieces of pond weed 15 cm long

  Here are their results.

Student	Number of bubbles of oxygen
1	17
2	13
3	12
4	14
5	14

a Name one other process which affects the rate of oxygen release

from plants? ___Temperature___ [1]

b Suggest **three** reasons why the number of bubbles varied.

  The temperature was not constant.

  Carbon Dioxide levels varied

  Light's distance may be different [3]

c Suggest **how** a class can combine their results for this experiment.

  Calculate an average [1]

d Explain **why** the class should combine the results.

  To get reliable results. To obtain

  variables

  [3]

Total [8]

2 Look at the graph.

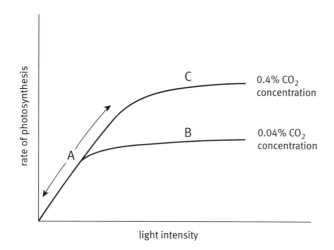

light intensity

a Match the letters on the graph to these labels.

Photosynthesis is increasing at the highest rate. A

Carbon dioxide is limiting the rate of photosynthesis. B

Extra carbon dioxide has increased the rate of photosynthesis. C [3]

b Carbon dioxide and light levels affect the rate of photosynthesis.

Write down **one** other factor that could affect the rate. Temperature [1]

Total [4]

3 The graph shows changes in the rate of photosynthesis over 24 hours.

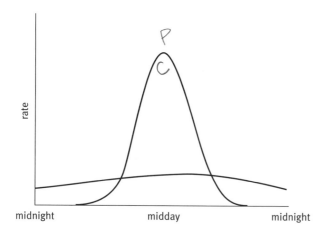

midnight   midday   midnight

a Only one of the graph lines shows the rate of photosynthesis. Label it P.

Give a reason for your choice.

It shows During midday it's highest. [2]

H **b** Label a compensation point C. [1]

c Compare the movement of carbon dioxide into or out of the plant at a compensation point.

It's the same [1]

Total [4]

4 Scientists obtained the data in the graphs on page 108 from Antarctic ice cores up to 160 thousand years old.

a What is the range of temperature shown on graph B? _+8_ ~~2+6=8~~ [1]

b What does graph B show about the average temperature of Antarctica over the past 160 thousand years?

The temp dramatically decreased, and is now steadily increasing [1]

c Does the graph provide evidence for global warming? _A_

Explain your answer.

It shows that CO_2 levels are rising, and CO_2 damages the ozone layer causing global warming [3]

d The greenhouse effect is the increase in the average temperature of the Earth due to increasing concentrations of 'greenhouse gases' such as carbon dioxide and methane. Describe one piece of evidence for the 'greenhouse effect' that the graphs show.

The graphs show that the higher the methane and CO_2 levels, the higher the temperature. [2]

e Most scientists agree that human activity is increasing the amount of carbon dioxide in the air. But they think that there is no evidence on these graphs for the idea that human activity is the cause. Explain why.

It does not show the source which emits the CO_2 or methane, therefore it is not sure whether humans are to blame. [2]

Total [9]

A

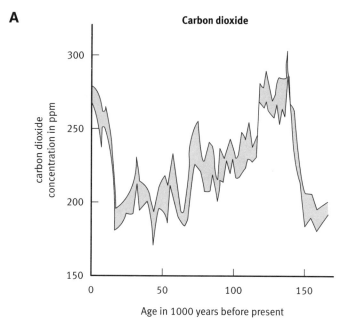

Carbon dioxide

B

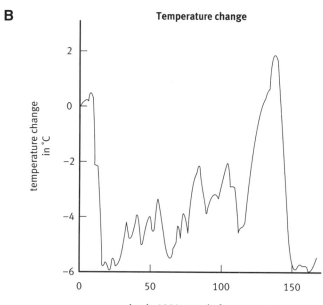

Temperature change

C

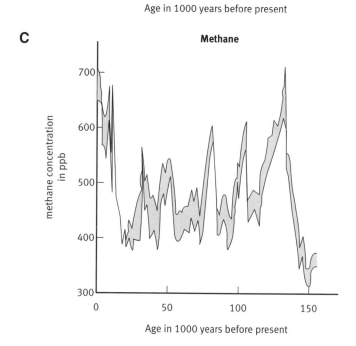

Methane

1 Draw lines to match the **definitions**, **types of associations** and **examples** of feeding relationships.

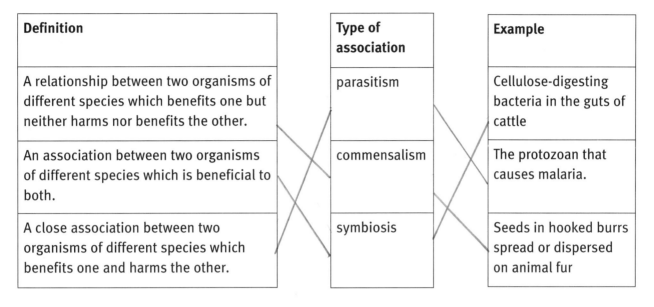

Definition	Type of association	Example
A relationship between two organisms of different species which benefits one but neither harms nor benefits the other.	parasitism	Cellulose-digesting bacteria in the guts of cattle
An association between two organisms of different species which is beneficial to both.	commensalism	The protozoan that causes malaria.
A close association between two organisms of different species which benefits one and harms the other.	symbiosis	Seeds in hooked burrs spread or dispersed on animal fur

2 Complete the sentences in the speech bubbles. Choose from these words. You can use the words once, more than once, or not at all.

blood	sneezing	food	less	urine	malnutrition
more	headaches	mosquitoes		temperature	yield

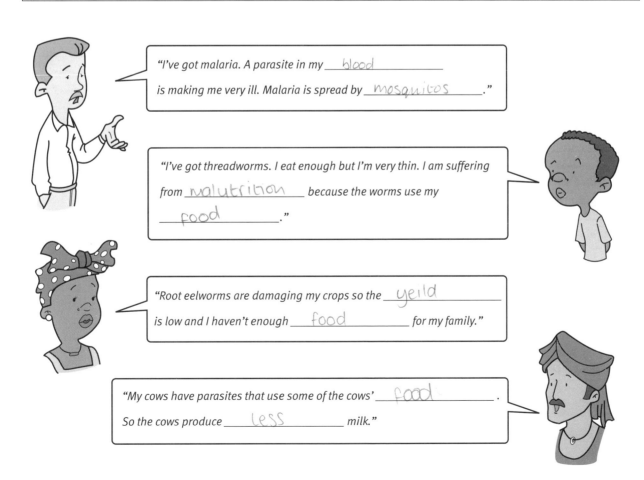

"I've got malaria. A parasite in my ___blood___
is making me very ill. Malaria is spread by ___mosquitos___."

"I've got threadworms. I eat enough but I'm very thin. I am suffering
from ___malutrition___ because the worms use my
___food___."

"Root eelworms are damaging my crops so the ___yeild___
is low and I haven't enough ___food___ for my family."

"My cows have parasites that use some of the cows' ___food___.
So the cows produce ___less___ milk."

3 What is the cause of sickle-cell anaemia? Choose from:

a parasite in the blood ☐

a bacterial infection ☐

a faulty recessive allele ☑

a faulty dominant allele ☐

4 Parasites only survive because they are adapted to find a host and to live in or on their hosts. Complete the table with the correct adaptation.

Adaptations:

▶ produces large numbers of eggs
▶ use anaerobic respiration
▶ thick, enzyme-resistant cuticle
▶ male and female sex organs
▶ suckers and stickers on head

I live in the human gut, so I've got problems!

My problem	My solution
Contractions of the gut wall try to push me out.	Suckers and stickers on head
Digestive enzymes in the gut could harm me.	thick, enzyme-resistant cuticle
There's little or no oxygen inside the gut.	use anaerobic respiration
I live on my own so I haven't a mate.	male + female sex organs
I can produce eggs on my own, but the chances of them finding the next host are small.	produces large numbers of eggs

5 The statements below are parts of the life cycle of a tapeworm.
Number them in the order they happen.

1   adult tapeworm in the gut   ◀———————— start here

4   egg hatches in a pig's muscle

6   tapeworm develops in human intestine

3   eggs eaten by a pig

2   eggs released into faeces

5   human eats undercooked pork

Recognising different associations of organisms

Corals and the green algae in their cells benefit each other. So we say that they have a **symbiotic** relationship.

An orchid attached to the branch of a tree does the tree no harm. But the orchid benefits by getting more light. So this is an example of **commensalism**.

Parasitism is a close association between two organisms of different species which is beneficial to one (the **parasite**) and harmful to the other (the **host**). Examples are tapeworms and the malaria parasite.

How do parasites survive?

Parasites have to be adapted for finding a host and for living in or on their host.

The evolution of a parasite is thought to be closely linked to the evolution of its host.

Tapeworms

- have suckers and/or hooks to grip the gut wall
- have a thick cuticle to resist enzymes
- can respire anaerobically so they can manage without oxygen
- have male and female sex organs so they can reproduce without a mate
- produce lots of eggs to increase the chances of eggs finding a new host

Malaria parasites

- are spread to new hosts by mosquitoes
- live inside red blood cells for most of the time that they are in the blood; so they are protected from the immune system
- have different surface markers at different stages of their lifecycle; this prevents white blood cells from recognizing them

Parasites cause problems such as:

- human diseases, including malaria
- reduced food yields (both plants and animals)

H Sickle-cell anaemia is caused by a faulty recessive allele that codes for haemoglobin. Some of the red blood cells go out of shape causing these symptoms:

- severe pain, when sickled red blood cells block tiny blood vessels
- anaemia as damaged cells can't be replaced fast enough
- tiredness caused by shortage of oxygen

However people who carry just one sickle-cell allele are less likely to get malaria. They have an improved chance of survival. So, the frequency of the sickle-cell allele has increased in places where malaria is a problem. This is an example of natural selection.

1 **a** Explain the term parasitism.

<u>Where 1 organism benefits, and</u>
<u>+ harms it</u> [2]

b Look at the relationships in this list.

Tick **two** that are parasitic. Draw a ring around **two** that are symbiotic.

✓threadworms feeding on digested food in human guts

nitrogen-fixing bacteria in the root nodules of legumes

✓ivy growing on a tree and sucking nutrients from it

clown fish protected by a giant anemone and scattering food particles which the anenome eats [4]

c Write down **two** adaptations that make the malaria parasite a success.

<u>different markers during life cycle</u>
<u>lives in red blood cells.</u> [2]

d Write down **three** problems caused by parasites.

<u>Diseases - malaria</u>
<u>Decreased crop yield</u>
<u>Slowed growth of farm animals</u> [3]

Total [11]

2 Complete the table:

Relationship name	Description of relationship	Example of relationship
parasitism	1 organism harms the other	mosquito + human
Symbiotic	both organisms benefit	coral + Algae
commensalism	one organism benefits and the other is unharmed	orchid + tree

Total [4]

3 A population of malaria parasites can evolve when white blood cells learn to recognize a particular surface marker. For these sentences, write down the letters A–G in the order that shows how this change happens.

A White blood cells recognize a common surface marker on malaria parasites.

B A few have different surface markers.

C The surface markers on malaria parasites vary.

D They destroy these parasites.

E The white blood cells don't recognize them.

F A different surface marker is now common.

G These survive and reproduce.

C,  A, D, B, E, G, F   **Total [5]**

H **4** The sickle-cell allele is recessive so only people with two sickle-cell alleles have the disorder. This is the inheritance pattern.

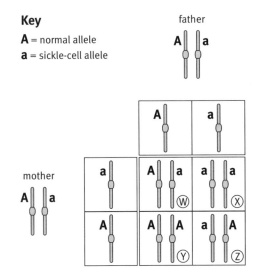

a Which child, **W**, **X**, **Y** or **Z** has sickle-cell disorder?

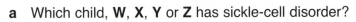

_____ A _____ [1]

b Describe **one** effect of this disorder on the child.

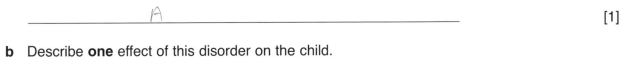

_____ tiredness _____ [1]

c People who are carriers of sickle-cell anaemia are less likely to get malaria than people who don't have that allele.

Which **two** do **not** have sickle-cell disorder, but have some protection from malaria? Choose from **W**, **X**, **Y** or **Z**.

_____ W, Z _____ [1]

d Look at the maps.

Distribution of malaria in Africa

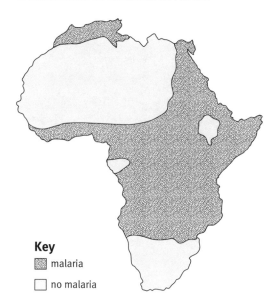

Key
▨ malaria
☐ no malaria

Frequency of the sickle-cell allele

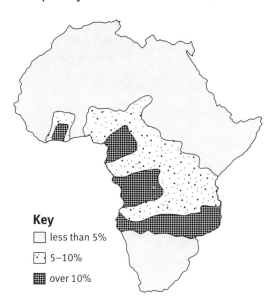

Key
☐ less than 5%
⊡ 5–10%
▦ over 10%

What is the relationship between the distribution of sickle-cell disorder and malaria?

The places where there is malaria, there is sickle cell disorder.

[2]

e Explain **how** the sickle-cell allele increased in frequency in malaria areas.

The sickle cell allele meant that they did not have malaria, and therefore did not die. This means that the sickle cell people can survive to reproduce and pass on that allele to their offspring.

[4]

f Write down the name of the process you described in **e**. [1]

Natural Selection.

Total [10]

1 Which of the cells, **A** to **D**, is a bacterial cell? _C_

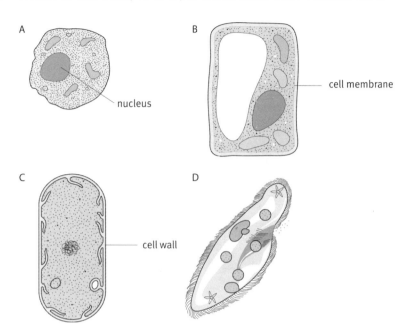

2 The words in the grid are all words that you used in this topic. Complete the grid. Another word should appear in the shaded column. Make up your own clue for this word.

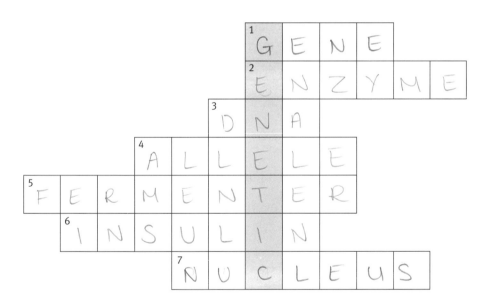

Clues across:

1 a section of a chromosome that controls a particular characteristic

2 a protein that catalyses chemical reactions in cells

3 the chemical that makes up chromosomes

4 a form of a gene

5 a vessel in which we grow microorganisms on a large scale

6 a human hormone produced by genetically modified bacteria

7 the part of a cell that contains the chromosomes

Your clue: _Genetic_

3

Example of genetically modified organism (GMO)	Benefit
1. Scientists transferred the human insulin gene to bacteria. These bacteria, grown in a fermenter, produce human insulin.	Diabetics can use human insulin made by bacteria instead of using animal insulin.
2. Genetically modified yeast produces the rennet we use for making vegetarian cheese.	Rennet from calves' stomachs is no longer essential for cheese-making.
3. A gene for herbicide resistance from a bacterium was transferred into sugar beet.	This GM sugar beet is not killed by the weed-killer 'Roundup'.
4. Scientists cancelled out the gene for an enzyme that makes tomatoes soften as they ripen.	This made the fruit more resistant to rot so they keep for longer.
5. A gene for increasing vitamin A production was added to rice. The modified rice is called 'Golden Rice'.	This can reduce the vitamin A deficiency that causes eyesight problems, including blindness.
6. A gene for a pesticide was transferred from a bacterium into corn.	This reduces damage by the insects that feed on corn. Yields increase.

On the chart:

a Underline an animal gene transferred to bacteria.

b Draw a ring around a bacterial gene transferred to a plant.

c Draw a box around a GM plant that may help to prevent blindness.

d Draw a star next to an example of a gene being lost not added.

e Write F in the margin next to **two** genetically modified organisms that are grown in a fermenter.

f Write Y in the margin next to **two** examples in which genetic modification has increased crop yield.

4 Fill in the missing words in the cartoons.

Use these words:

chemical	different	gene	insect	nuclei	plants

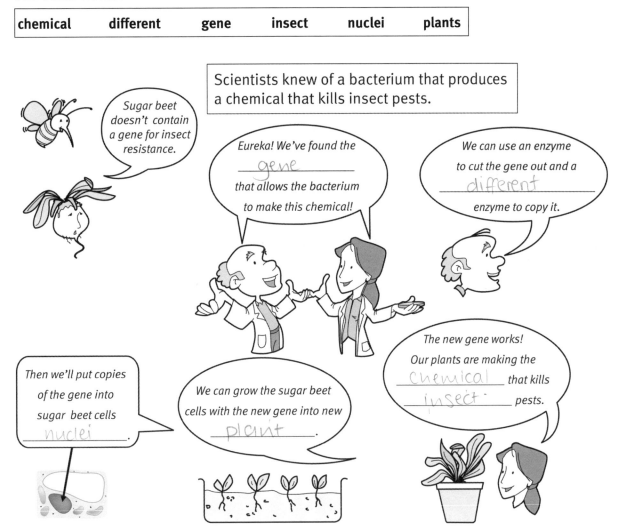

Scientists knew of a bacterium that produces a chemical that kills insect pests.

Sugar beet doesn't contain a gene for insect resistance.

Eureka! We've found the _gene_ that allows the bacterium to make this chemical!

We can use an enzyme to cut the gene out and a _different_ enzyme to copy it.

Then we'll put copies of the gene into sugar beet cells _nuclei_.

We can grow the sugar beet cells with the new gene into new _plant_.

The new gene works! Our plants are making the _chemical_ that kills _insect_ pests.

5 People at risk of a genetic disorder may have a test to find out if they have the faulty allele for the gene. This allele may affect them in later life, or it could be passed on to children.

a These are the steps in carrying out a genetic test.

Number them to show the correct order.

Use gentle heat to separate the two strands of the DNA.	5	5
Use enzymes to cut up the DNA.	4	4
Produce a gene probe for the allele.	1	
Use UV or autoradiography to locate gene probe.	7	7
Extract DNA from white blood cells.	3	3
Take a blood sample and separate out the white blood cells.	2	2
Add the gene probe to the DNA fragments	6	6

Use this gene probe to find out whether or not either of these people is a carrier of cystic fibrosis.

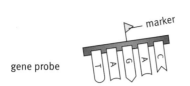

gene probe

marker

A – T
C – G

BOB'S DNA   SALLY'S DNA

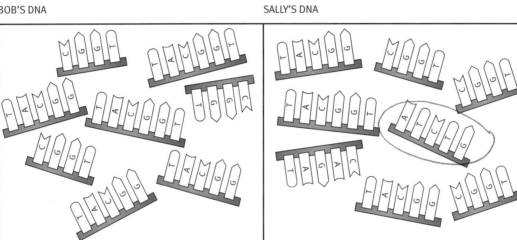

ATCTG

<u>Sally's a carrier</u>

What is the structure of bacteria?

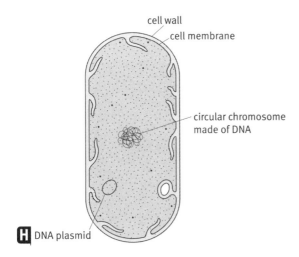

cell wall

cell membrane

circular chromosome made of DNA

H DNA plasmid

What can we make using microorganisms?

We can grow bacteria and fungi on a large scale in **fermenters**.
We call the process **fermentation**.

Products made this way include:

▸ antibiotics

▸ single-cell protein; microbes grown for food

▸ enzymes for food manufacture,
for example, rennin for making cheese

Some of these are made using genetically modified microorganisms.

How are cells genetically modified?

When scientists genetically modify an organism, they alter or modify its characteristics by transferring genes from another organism into its DNA.

Scientists:

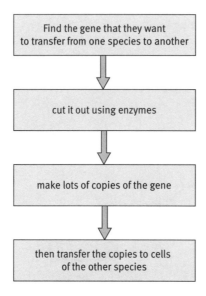

H N.B. They use a vector (carrier), a virus or a plasmid, to transfer the genes.

Some examples of genetic modification are:

▸ modifying microorganisms for making
– drugs such as improved forms of antibiotics
– hormones such as insulin

▸ modifying crop plants to make them resistant to pests and diseases

Remember that you need to be able to discuss some of the economic, social and ethical implications for the release of genetically modified organisms into the environment.

Economical
– cheap

Social
– People should have a choice

Ethical
– morally wrong to alter DNA

How can we use DNA technology in genetic testing?

Scientists can use genetic testing to identify faulty alleles in

▶ adults
▶ fetuses
▶ IVF embryos

Disorders that they can identify include cystic fibrosis and Huntington's disorder. They use a special piece of DNA called a gene probe. This is a single strand of DNA with bases that will pair with the faulty allele.

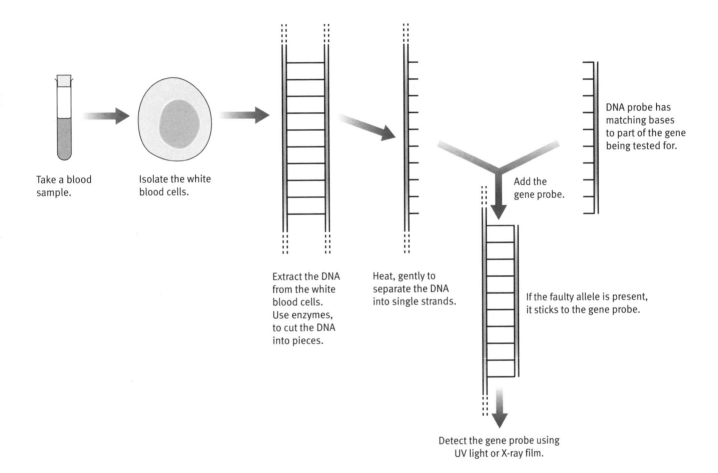

Take a blood sample.

Isolate the white blood cells.

Extract the DNA from the white blood cells. Use enzymes, to cut the DNA into pieces.

Heat, gently to separate the DNA into single strands.

Add the gene probe.

DNA probe has matching bases to part of the gene being tested for.

If the faulty allele is present, it sticks to the gene probe.

Detect the gene probe using UV light or X-ray film.

1 Write down

   a **two** groups of organisms that we can grow in a fermenter

     bacteria and _yeast_ [2]

   b **two** useful products that we obtain by fermentation

     alcohol and _penicillin_ [2]

                                                          Total [4]

2 For **one** example of the genetic modification of a crop plant, write down

   a the name of the crop _bacteria_ [1]

   b the name of the organism from which the gene is transferred

     humans [1]

   c the purpose of the gene transfer

     insulin to treat diabetes [1]

                                                           Total [3]

3 Genetic modification involves:

   ▸ isolating and replicating a gene from one species

   ▸ transferring copies of the gene into the cells of a different species

     a What does the word 'replicating' mean? _altering_ [1]

     b Scientists use one enzyme to cut up DNA and a different enzyme
     for replicating DNA. Explain why they use two different enzymes.

       They take the useful gene, and place

                                                      [1]

                                                           Total [2]

H **4** **a** What is the purpose of a vector in genetic modification?

     It can reproduce [1]

   b Write down **two** kinds of vectors.

     virus and _plasmid_ [2]

                                                          Total [3]

5 **a** A gene probe is composed of **two** parts: DNA and a marker.

There are two types of marker.

i Is the DNA in a gene probe a single or a double strand?

_____Single_____

ii What **two** different ways do we use to show up the two different

types of marker?

_____UV_____ and _____X-ray film_____ [3]

b Choose a particular gene probe. Describe what scientists use that
gene probe for.

_____

_____ [2]

c Explain how they use the gene probe.

_____

_____

_____ [3]

Total [8]

6 These are some comments about food from genetically modified organisms.

A **Some people say ...**	**B** **Others say ...**
We don't want genes from animals or from nuts in our food.	Our research shows that any genes transferred stay in the environment for no more than four years.
The added pesticides in the plants could harm us.	GM crops give us higher crop yields so they will help to feed people in the developing world.
Many farmers in developing countries save their own seed and can't afford expensive GM seed.	Genetically modified food is safe. It is the same as any other.
Pollen from GM crops may pollinate related wild plants or nearby non-GM plants spreading the added gene throughout the environment.	✓ We use fewer pesticides when we grow plants that produce their own pesticides.
Non-GM crops do get contaminated with GM crops after harvest. Hardly any soya from the USA is free of GM beans.	It doesn't matter where the transferred gene comes from. All organisms use the same genetic code.

a Suggest the type of organisation or person likely to make the comments in

  i column A

  Environmentalist

  ii column B

  Charity   [2]

b In column A, find the statement, 'The added pesticides in the plants could harm us.'

  In column B, find and tick the **best** counter-argument to this statement.   [1]

c Suggest why some people may not want, in their food, genes from

  i nuts

_____ allergic _____

  ii any animals

_____ vegetarian _____

  iii certain animals

_____ religious fest reasons _____ [3]

d Column B sets out some benefits of the genetic modification of food crops.

  Write down **two** reasons why some people think that GM is unethical.

Genes are altered - not natural

Food has a mixture of organisms. [2]

e In column B, there is the claim that GM food is safe.

  i Write down **one** possible risk to the environment of growing GM crops.

Pesticides can get into food chains

  ii Some people think that we shouldn't grow GM crops because of this risk. They say we should use the 'precautionary principle'.

  Explain the precautionary principle.

If the action produces more harm

than benefit, then it should not be done. [3]

Total [11]

1 Fill in the blanks. Choose from these words.

You may use each word once, more than once, or not at all.

aerobic	air	anaerobic	blood	cells	citric	down
energy	equation	faster	glucose	lactic	lungs	muscles
organisms	oxygen	quickly	slowly	up	anaerobically	

To contract, ~~the~~ _muscles_ need energy from respiration.

Your cells need _oxygen_ for respiration. You get oxygen from the _air_ that you breathe into your _lungs_. You breathe more _quic_ when you exercise.

Your heart pumps _blood_ containing oxygen to your tissues. When you exercise your heart beats more _faster_.

During exercise cells respire _faster_ to provide additional _energy_ for movement.

anaerobic → lactic acid (+ _glucose_ released)

Anaerobic respiration in animals is summarized by this _equation_ .

Sometimes the amount of _oxygen_ reaching the muscles is too low. Then the muscle _cells_ use ~~anen~~ _anaerobic_ respiration. The waste product _lactic_ acid builds up in the _muscles_ .

H _aerobic_ respiration releases more energy from a glucose molecule than _anaerobic_ respiration. However, when cells are short of oxygen, anaerobic respiration is of benefit to humans and other _organisms_ . Humans need _oxygen_ to break down the lactic acid in muscle cells. The amount needed is called the _oxygen_ debt. The breakdown of the lactic acid releases more _energy_ .

2 Draw a ring around the correct word or words from each of the pairs shown in bold.

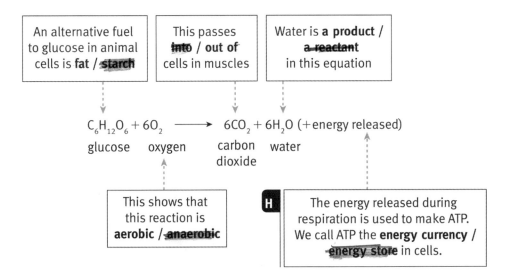

An alternative fuel to glucose in animal cells is **fat / ~~starch~~**

This passes **~~into~~ / out of** cells in muscles

Water is **a product / ~~a reactant~~** in this equation

$$C_6H_{12}O_6 + 6O_2 \longrightarrow 6CO_2 + 6H_2O \ (+\text{energy released})$$

glucose   oxygen   carbon   water
                        dioxide

This shows that this reaction is **aerobic / ~~anaerobic~~**

H The energy released during respiration is used to make ATP. We call ATP the **energy currency / ~~energy store~~** in cells.

3 The words in the grid are all words that you used in this topic. Complete the grid.

Another word should appear in the shaded column. Make up your own clue for this word.

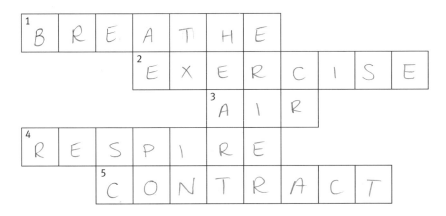

1	B	R	E	A	T	H	E
			2	E	X	E	R	C	I	S	E
				3	A	I	R
4	R	E	S	P	I	R	E
		5	C	O	N	T	R	A	C	T

Clues:

1 You do this to move gas in and out of your lungs.

2 This causes an increase in breathing rate and depth – and it's good for you!

3 This goes in and out of your lungs.

4 What cells do to release energy.

5 Muscles do this to make parts of the body move.

Your clue: _____Heart_____

What is aerobic respiration?

Aerobic respiration happens in cells. In aerobic respiration:

▶ oxygen is used
▶ energy is released from food chemicals such as glucose

The equation is:

glucose + oxygen → carbon dioxide + water (+ energy released)

What happens to the energy released?

The energy released in respiration is used for life processes including movement. It is the energy from respiration that enables muscles to contract.

H The energy released during respiration is first used to make a chemical called ATP. The energy for the contraction of muscle tissue comes directly from the breakdown of ATP. We call ATP the 'energy currency' of living things.

When you exercise, your muscle cells respire faster to provide additional energy for movement. So, they need an increase in the rate of:

▶ oxygen supply
▶ glucose supply
▶ carbon dioxide removal

That is why your heart and breathing rates increase during exercise.

Because factors such as heart rate vary, 'normal' measurements are given within a range.

What is anaerobic respiration?

This is the kind of respiration that takes place in muscle cells when they don't get enough oxygen. It is a way of releasing energy without oxygen.

The word equation for anaerobic respiration in human body cells is

glucose → lactic acid (+ energy released*)

* aerobic respiration releases more energy per glucose molecule than anaerobic respiration

In anaerobic respiration, lactic acid builds up in muscles. It makes them feel sore and tired.

H Oxygen is needed to break down the lactic acid and release the energy left in it. The amount of oxygen needed is called the 'oxygen debt'. However, when there is a shortage of oxygen, anaerobic respiration is beneficial for human beings and other organisms.

1 a Write down the word equation for aerobic respiration.

glucose + oxygen ⟶ water + carbon Dioxide [2]

b Write down **two** similarities between aerobic and anaerobic respiration.

Both needs glucose

Both produces energy. [2]

c Write down **two** differences between aerobic and anaerobic respiration.

anaerobic = lactic acid

aerobic = carbon dioxide + water [2]

d Where does aerobic and anaerobic respiration take place?

muscle cells [1]

Total [7]

2 During exercise, muscle cells require more oxygen to release more energy during respiration.

a Write down **two** changes in the body that increase oxygen uptake.

increased heart rate + breathing. [2]

b Muscles use the energy to do work.

What do muscles do to cause movement? *contract* [1]

Total [3]

3 The graph shows Donna's rate of oxygen uptake during and after exercise.

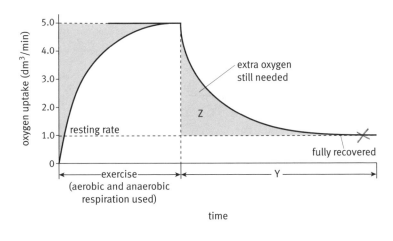

a i Write an **X** on the graph to show when Donna stopped exercising. [1]

ii Donna uses oxygen to release energy in respiration when she is resting.

Write down **two** uses of this energy.

Oxygen debt.

Break down lactic acid to produce energy [2]

b **i** **Z** represents the extra oxygen Donna's muscles are still using after exercise.

What do we call the amount of extra oxygen needed?

Oxygen debt [1]

ii Explain, as fully as you can, what Donna's cells are using this extra oxygen for.

The extra oxygen is used to break down the lactic acid produced in anaerobic respiration. Energy will be produced when lactic acid is broken down [2]

c Name the energy-rich chemical that we call the 'energy currency'

of cells. _ATP_ [1]

d Name the process that results in the production of this chemical.

Respiration [1]

Total [8]

4 A group of students investigated heart rates. The table shows their results.

Name	Pete	Bill	Ali	Leah	Bob	Jason	Col	Tai	Sue	Liam
Heart rate before exercise	72	58	70	71	80	83	90	77	64	69
Heart rate after exercise	75	91	111	106	118	122	78	105	117	125

a What is the range of heart rates before exercise? _32_ [1]

b Why did the heart rates of the students vary?

individual's fitness levels. [1]

c Work out the average heart rate before exercise.

_73.4_ [2]

d What pattern do the data show?

Your heart rate increases after you have done exercise. [1]

e i Col's result is odd. What do we call figures that don't fit the pattern?

anomaly.

ii Suggest **two** possible reasons for this odd result.

- MIS-counted heart rate

- wrote down results incorrectly. [3]

f One person hid instead of exercising. Suggest who it was (Do not include COL.).

Pete

Give a reason for your suggestion.

Not a big range between heart rates [2]

Total [10]

1 Look at the diagram of some of the components of blood. Then complete the table.

A   B   C

Component	What it is	Its function
A	red bloodcell	transport oxygen
B	white bloodcell	fight off infection
C	Platelet	Help clot blood

2 Complete the sentences by crossing out the bold words that are incorrect.

Blood contains antigens and antibodies. **Antigens / ~~antibodies~~** are markers on the surface of foreign cells; including the surface of **red / ~~white~~** blood cells. **~~Antigens~~ / antibodies** are substances in blood plasma. They are made by **~~red~~ / white** blood cells and they destroy foreign cells.

3 You cannot have antibodies to the antigens in your own blood.

This information should help you to complete the table and the sentences.

Blood type	Antigens	Antibodies
A	A	Anti B
B	B	Anti A
AB	A and B	none
O	neither	Anti A + Anti B

In blood transfusions, if people receive blood of the wrong type, their antibodies 'clot' the donor's cells. The clots block their blood vessels, stopping blood flow. Before people knew about blood types, many people died as a result.

Which group of people didn't die as a result of transfusion?
Blood type ___ AB

Explain why: __it can recieve any blood donation__ .No
Anti A or Anti B antibodies .

H **4** True or false?

    a Three genes determine your ABO blood type.   T /(F) ✓

    b Two of the blood type alleles are codominant.   (T)/ F ✓

    c The blood type O allele is dominant.   T /(F) ✓

    d The blood type A allele is dominant.   (T)/F

    e Each person has only two of the blood type alleles.   (T)/ F

    f A person cannot have two recessive blood type alleles.   (T)/F

5 **a** Draw a ring around **one** mistake in each genetic diagram.

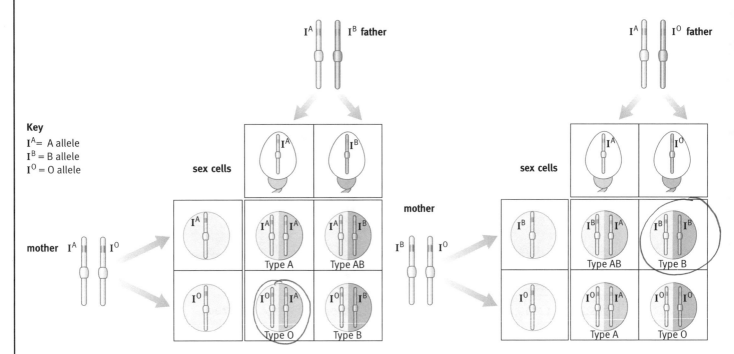

Key
I^A = A allele
I^B = B allele
I^0 = O allele

    b Complete a genetic diagram for parents who are BB and AB using only letters A and B.

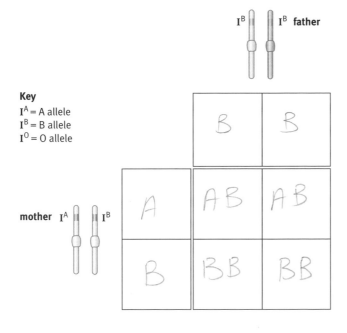

Key
I^A = A allele
I^B = B allele
I^0 = O allele

6 **a** Use the letters **A** to **F** to label the diagram of a human heart:

    A the left atrium

    B a ventricle

    C the main artery to the body

    D a vein from the body

    E a vein from the lungs

    F two different types of valves that prevent backflow of blood

  b Draw arrows to show the direction of blood flow through the heart and blood vessels.

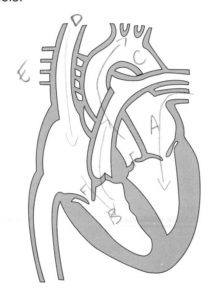

7 **a** Complete the sentences using the following words:

pass	**carbon dioxide**	**glucose**	**capillary**	**dissolved**
pressure	**one**	**urea**		

Exchanges between your blood and your cells happen in

_____capillary_____ networks.

The walls of these blood vessels are only _____one_____ cell thick.

Water and _dissolved_____ substances are squeezed out of

these vessels as a result of high blood _pressure_____ .

The concentration of substances such as oxygen and

_____glucose_____ is lower in the cells than in this fluid.

So they _____pass_____ into the cells. Two waste products that

pass from the cells into the blood are _____carbon_____

_____dioxide____ and _____urea_____ .

b Complete the labels by crossing out the bold words that are incorrect.

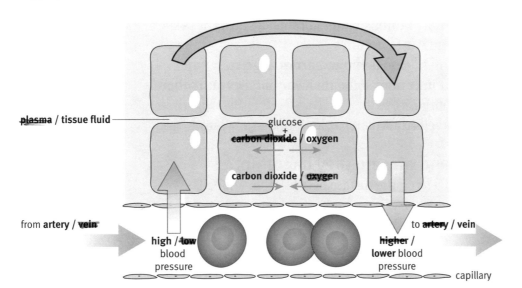

plasma / tissue fluid

glucose
+
carbon dioxide / oxygen

carbon dioxide / oxygen

from **artery** / **vein**

high / **low** blood pressure

to **artery** / vein

higher / **lower** blood pressure

capillary

What is in blood?

Human blood contains:

- a fluid called plasma – that contains water, dissolved substances such as glucose, hormones and waste products
- red blood cells containing haemoglobin to carry oxygen
- white blood cells to fight infection; some make antibodies and others engulf and digest microorganisms
- platelets – fragments of cells that help to clot blood at a wound

What are blood types and why are they important?

There are markers called antigens on the surface of cells. If an antibody recognizes a foreign antigen, it joins with it. Antibodies destroy cells in various ways.

If a person receiving a blood transfusion (the recipient) has antibodies to the antigens on the donor's red blood cells:

- the red blood cells clump together
- they block blood vessels and the person dies

So, to avoid clotting, the donor and recipient's blood must be matched.

antibody ——

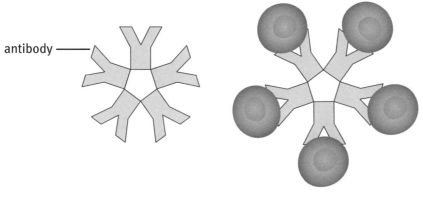

The free ends of antibodies to red blood cell antigens can attach themselves to five red blood cells.

The red blood cells clump together.

How do we know which blood is safe?

Remember that the recipient's blood must not contain antibodies to the donor's cells.

Blood type	Antigens on the cells	Antibodies	So, this will clot blood type . . .	Can receive blood type. . .
A	A	Anti-B	B	A or O
B	B	Anti-A	A	B or O
AB	AB	None	None	AB, A, B, O
O	Neither	Anti-A and Anti-B	A, B and AB	O

So, people with type AB blood (**universal recipients**) can receive blood from anyone.

The red cells in type O blood have no antigens so anyone can safely receive type O blood. So we call people with type O blood **universal donors**.

What is your heart like?

Your heart pumps blood into arteries. Blood circulates:

heart → artery → smaller arteries → capillaries → small veins → veins → heart

In one circulation around the body, the blood flows through your heart twice. We call this the **double circulation**. We need it so that the blood:

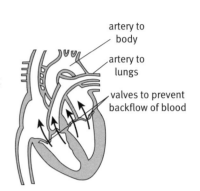

▸ gains oxygen and loses carbon dioxide in the circulation through the lungs
▸ loses oxygen and gains waste carbon dioxide as it circulates around the rest of the body

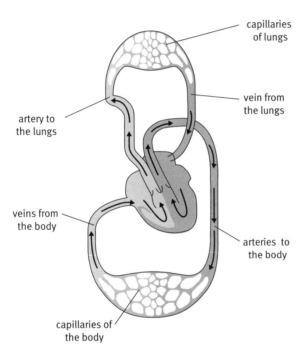

Double circulation – simplified

Why are capillaries important?

Capillary walls are only one cell thick, so:

▸ Blood pressure can force water and dissolved substances from the blood out into the tissues. This forms tissue fluid
▸ Substances such as oxygen, carbon dioxide, glucose and urea can diffuse between the blood and the tissues.

1 **a** When you have a blood transfusion, it is important that you receive blood of the correct group. What are the **four** blood groups in the ABO blood type system?

A, B, AB, O

[2]

b What happens if a person receives a blood transfusion of the wrong blood group? Explain your answer.

The ~~blood~~ body will reject the blood as the body thinks it is a foreigner, and so antibodies clumps the blood, and blood clots.

[3]

c Complete the table to show which blood types are a safe match for transfusion. [8]

Recipient / Donor	O anti-A + anti-B	A anti-B	B anti-A	*AB none
O anti-A + anti-B				
A anti-B				
B anti-A				
AB none				

Key
− no clotting
* clotting

Total [13]

H **2** **a** In the ABO blood type system:

    i how many genes are involved? ____1____

    ii which allele is recessive? ____O____

    iii two alleles are codominant. What does codominant mean?

      ____Both are dominant. Both will show up____

b Complete the diagram for parents AA and BO.   [12]

                                                                                Total [15]

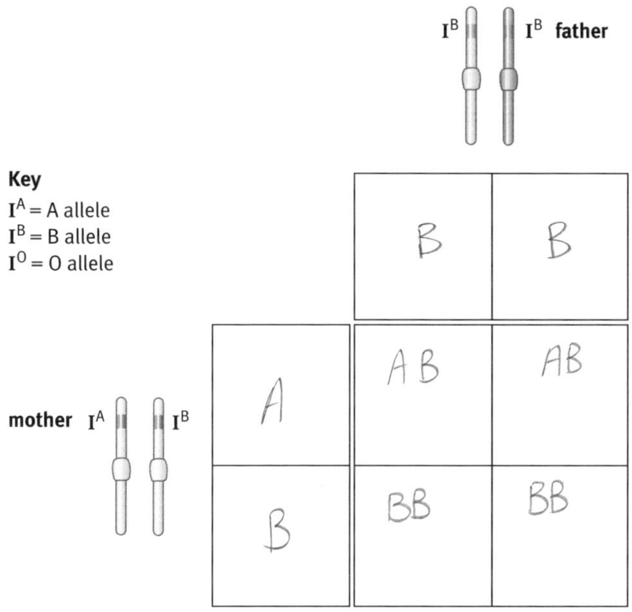

I^B I^B **father**

Key
I^A = A allele
I^B = B allele
I^O = O allele

mother I^A I^B

	B	B
A	A B	AB
B	BB	BB

3 a Your heart has a double circulatory system. Explain how this helps to ensure that only
deoxygenated blood goes to the lungs.

_____

_____

_____   [2]

b Which type of blood cell becomes oxygenated in the lungs? <u>red   blood cell.</u>   [1]

c Explain these features of the heart and circulation:

i The left ventricle wall is thicker than the right ventricle wall.

<u>Left ventricle pumps blood to body,</u>
<u>meaning more pressure and</u>
<u>energy needed.</u>

ii All veins have valves.

<u>To ensure blood does not travel</u>
<u>the other way.</u>

_____

iii Arteries have valves only where they leave the heart.

<u>So blood can't travel the other</u>
<u>way (backwards).</u>

_____

iv Arteries have thicker walls than veins.

<u>The pressure is higher and</u>
<u>has more energy to pump blood</u>
<u>to rest of body.</u>

v Capillary networks are very important.

<u>lets oxygen etc diffuse between</u>
<u>blood + tissue.</u>   [10]

Total [13]

1 Complete the speech bubbles.

I've got tennis elbow.

Extra synovial *fluid in the joint is making it painful.*

My knee hurts. The bones are rubbing together because I've damaged the cartilage. *at the ends of the bones.*

I've sprained my ankle. I overstretched the ligament *when I fell.*

My arm bone has come out of its socket. The joint is dislocated.

2 Suggest **two** exercises that Anna can do to get her ankle moving more easily after the swelling of her ankle has gone down.

flexing ankle joint.

Gentle exercises.

3 True or false?

a	Relaxation of muscles makes bones move.	**T /F** ✓
b	Ligaments join muscles to bones.	**T /F** ✓
c	Muscles work in pairs called antagonistic pairs.	**T/ F** ✓
d	Both muscles of an antagonistic pair contract at the same time.	**T /F** ✓
e	There are tendons at both ends of your biceps muscle.	**T /F** ✗
f	Your skeleton is only for support.	**T /F** ✓
g	Ligaments are made of tough, elastic tissue.	**T/ F** ✓

4 In the right hand column of the table, write down the trainer's reason for asking each of the questions.

The trainer's question	Why she asked the question
How much exercise do you normally do?	See fitness levels what it is capable of.
Do you smoke?	Fitness level affected - health.
Do you drink alcohol and if so, how much?	Health. Fitness related.
Are you taking any medicines?	meds may impact exercise capability
Is there a family history of heart disease?	Assess risk.

How do our joints help us to move?

Vertebrates such as humans have an internal skeleton of bone and cartilage for

▶ support and
▶ movement

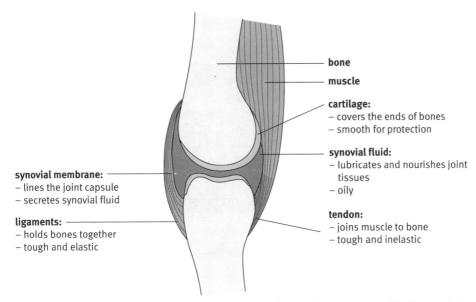

- **bone**
- **muscle**
- **cartilage:**
  – covers the ends of bones
  – smooth for protection
- **synovial fluid:**
  – lubricates and nourishes joint tissues
  – oily
- **tendon:**
  – joins muscle to bone
  – tough and inelastic
- **synovial membrane:**
  – lines the joint capsule
  – secretes synovial fluid
- **ligaments:**
  – holds bones together
  – tough and elastic

Notice that tissues in the joint have properties that make them suitable for the job they do.

Muscles can move bones at a joint only by contraction so they operate in antagonistic pairs. When one muscle of an antagonistic pair contracts, the other muscle relaxes.

How do we treat injuries to joints?

A lot of people injure themselves when they are exercising, particularly if they exercise excessively. Some common injuries are:

▶ sprains – overstretched ligaments
▶ dislocations – bones out of joint
▶ torn ligaments
▶ torn tendons

If you have sprained your ankle, it will be swollen, red or bruised looking and you will find walking difficult.

Treatment is

Rest – not moving the injured part

Ice – slows blood flow and reduces pain

Compress – bandage to reduce swelling

Elevate – raise to reduce blood flow and drain fluid

When the swelling has gone down you may need physiotherapy to get the joint and muscles moving again. Strengthening the muscles also reduces the risk of further injury.

Why do doctors and fitness trainers ask so many questions?

Some factors in your medical or lifestyle history that doctors need to know before they diagnose or treat a problem are:

▶ your symptoms
▶ your general health such as blood pressure
▶ any medication that you are already on
▶ any previous health problems or treatments
▶ your alcohol or tobacco consumption
▶ how much you exercise
▶ your family medical history

In the same way, a fitness trainer needs a lot of this information before you start a new exercise regime.

Both need the information:

▶ to ensure that what they suggest is safe for you.
▶ to plan a regime for you with realistic targets. The plan may be designed to cure you of a disease, improve your fitness or to get you back to normal after an injury or health problem (rehabilitation);
▶ as a baseline for monitoring your progress.

Keeping accurate records of progress is important. A treatment or an exercise plan may need to be changed because

▶ it isn't working;
▶ it's causing side effects.

In the case of side effects, treatment may be continued if the benefits are greater than the problems. However, there are often alternative treatments that can be tried.

H Doctors and trainers need to make sure that their way of monitoring their patient or client produces reliable data.

Following injury, muscles and joints need to be exercised to recover their strength and mobility. You need to be able to describe a set of exercises to treat an injury. This could include stretching the muscle, moving the joint without weight on it, and gentle exercise.

1   Simon joined a health club. The fitness trainer helped him to fill in a questionnaire about his health and lifestyle.

   a   Write down **two** reasons why the fitness trainer needed this information.

   To see whether he has previous medical
   problems. Also how much he exercise.   [2]

   b   List **five** health and lifestyle questions that a trainer is likely to ask a new client.

   Do you smoke?
   On meds?
   Family history of heart disease?
   Do you regularly exercise?
   Previous health problems.   [5]

   c   Six months later, the trainer asked Simon the same questions. Write down **two** reasons why he did this.

   make sure info is accurate.
   See what has changed.   [2]

   d   Write down **one** example of how a doctor could monitor a person's progress during and after treatment.

   During: _ask about reduction in symptoms._
   After: _measure blood levels for cholesteral._   [2]

   e   Write down **two** possible reasons for changing a three-month fitness programme after only one month.

   * Go easy
   * Injury - can't do it.   [2]

                                                                   Total [13]

2   His fitness trainer stored the data from Simon's health and lifestyle questionnaire.

   a   Write down **two** reasons why he needed to keep it.

   * To look back to see progress.
   * If he is benefitting from it.   [2]

   b   Write down **two** reasons why another fitness trainer might need to look at that data.

   * may want a second opinion
   * may take over the original trainer.   [2]

H

c The trainer checks Simon's progress every three months. For each assessment, he asks Simon to meet him at 10 a.m. and not to drink any coffee that morning. Suggest how that improves the reliability of the data about Simon's progress.

Everything is under the same conditions - fair test. Coffee ~~te~~ increases heart rate.

[2]

Total [6]

3 A sprain is a common injury that can be caused by excessive exercise.

a Write down **three** other injuries that can happen during exercise.

Dislocation of joints

torn ligaments

torn tendons.

[3]

b Describe the symptoms of a sprain.

Painful when try to use the joint.

Bruising. Walking difficult

[4]

c Write down **three** ways of reducing the swelling of a sprained ankle.

Rest

Rest - stop area being damaged more

Ice - ~~reduce~~ slow blood flow

Compression - reduce flow of blood

[3]

d In what **two** ways can physiotherapy speed up recovery following an injury?

* Gently exercise sprained area after swollen has gone.

* massage area to loosen muscles

[2]

Total [12]

4 **a** Label these parts on the diagram: [7]

cartilage ~~ligament~~ ~~muscle~~ ~~tendon~~ synovial fluid

~~synovial membrane~~

Muscle
tendon.
bone.
Synovial fluid
Synovial membrane.
cartilage.

b Ligaments are elastic and tendons are inelastic tissues because of the jobs they do.

Explain why:

i Ligaments need to be elastic.

So that ~~muscles~~ bones can move.

ii Tendons need to be inelastic.

bone and muscle are kept together, Muscle moves bone [4]

c Explain why muscles are in antagonistic pairs.

[3]

Total [14]

The scientific community

1

New research shows that the brainier male bats are, the smaller their testicles. Scientists studied 334 bat species, and found a correlation between brain size and testicle size: species with small brains have big testicles. The testicles of one bat species account for 8% of male bats' body mass. The scientists reported their findings in a **peer-reviewed scientific journal**.

2

So what do you think of that? That's equivalent to a man's testicles weighing about a stone! More than 6 kg! It can't be right, surely?

Well, the research is about bats – the scientists don't claim to have found out anything about men! But other scientists must have **evaluated** the claim, because the radio report said that the scientific journal is peer-reviewed.

3

Hmmm. It's a very new idea. I'm not sure I believe it.

I know what you mean. **Ideas that have been around longer are certainly more likely to be reliable**. For one thing, there's then been more time for the scientific community to evaluate the claims.

4

And do we know if anyone else has repeated the research?

Not as far as I know. If other scientists did a similar study, and the results were pretty much the same, then there'd be less reason to question their claim.
It would certainly be possible to try to **replicate the research** – the scientists reported exactly what they did very clearly.

THE HISTORY PROGRAMME
Presenters' script

23/08/2012

Presenter 1 (Simon)

Welcome to *The History Programme*. This year, 2012, is the hundredth anniversary of Wegener's theory of continental drift. We all now recognize the importance of his ideas. But a century ago scientists laughed at him.

Presenter 2 (Janet)

Yes, that's right. Wegener explained that the east coast of South America was once joined to Africa's west coast. The two continents had been slowly moving apart ever since. Wegener had lots of data to support his explanation: the shapes, rock types, fossils, and mountain ranges of the two continents matched up closely.

Presenter 1

So why did other scientists disagree with Wegener?

Presenter 2

Well, of course you can't simply deduce explanations from data. So it's quite reasonable for different scientists to come to different conclusions, even if they agree about some of the evidence. But there's more to it than that.

Presenter 1

Tell me more.

Presenter 2

It seems that other scientists simply couldn't imagine how massive continents could move across the planet. It was an **idea outside their experience**. Also, they didn't much respect Wegener – he was never regarded as a **member of the community of geologists**.

Presenter 1

And I suppose scientists don't give up their 'tried and tested' explanations easily?

Presenter 2

Exactly. Scientists often feel that it's safer to stick with **ideas that have served them well in the past**. Of course, new data that conflict with an explanation make scientists stop and think – but it could be that the data are incorrect, not the explanation! Generally, scientists only abandon an established explanation when there are really good reasons to do so, like someone suggesting a better one.

The scientific community

1 The stages below describe one way a scientific discovery is made and then accepted by other scientists.

They are in the wrong order.

A The scientist tells other scientists about the investigation results, either at a conference or in a scientific journal.

B Other scientists repeat the investigations.

C If their results are similar, the other scientists accept that the new idea is correct.

D Other scientists ask questions and evaluate the scientist's claims.

E A scientist makes an unexpected observation.

F The scientist does further investigations.

Fill in the boxes to show the right order. The first one has been done for you.

E					

2 Write a C next to reasons why two scientists may come to different conclusions about the same data.

Write an X next to reasons for scientists not abandoning an explanation even when new data do not seem to support the explanation.

a The scientists are interested in different areas of science.

b The data may be incorrect.

c The new explanation may run into problems.

d Different organizations paid for each scientist's research.

e It is safer to stick with ideas that have served well in the past.

3 Below are eight answers. Make up one question for each answer.

Peer review

_____

Scientific conference

_____

Other scientists get similar results.

_____

The explanation has stood the test of time.

_____

Scientific journal

_____

A tobacco company employs one scientist; a cancer charity employs the other scientist.

_____

New data may be inaccurate.

_____

Different sponsors have paid for the research.

_____

4 Read the information in the box.

> It's not only fatty foods and smoking that are risk factors for heart disease! New research shows that decaffeinated coffee may also be bad for your heart. American scientists studied 187 people for three months. They found increased levels of harmful cholesterol in the blood of people who drank decaffeinated coffee. The researchers presented their findings to other scientists at the American Heart Association's conference.

Make up a dialogue on page 155 to get across six important points about the scientific community.

Use the information in the box above and the phrases below.

- ▶ scientific journal or conference
- ▶ peer review
- ▶ evaluated by other scientists
- ▶ repeatable results
- ▶ different conclusions about the same data
- ▶ scientists not wanting to give up an explanation that has stood the test of time

The scientific community

1 Read the information.

> British scientists studied the effects of combinations of food additives on nerve cells.
> They used nerve cells from mice.
> They found that some combinations of food additives made the nerve cells stop growing.
> They found that the effects of combinations of additives were greater than the effects of single additives.
> They published their findings in a scientific journal.
> In the article, the scientists mentioned that food additives have been linked to behaviour problems in children.

a Why do scientists report their findings in scientific journals?
Tick the boxes next to the best answers.

to make sure their data is correct ☐

so that other scientists can repeat the research ☐

to make sure their research is reliable ☐

so that other scientists can evaluate the research ☐ [2]

b i A scientist reads the journal article carefully.
She wants to repeat the research.
Give one thing she needs to find out from the article before she can begin her experiment. Do not include things mentioned in the box above.

_____

_____ [1]

H

ii Why do scientists believe it is important to repeat experiments done by others?

To obtain To prove it is
possible to do. [1]

c   Other organizations commented on the research
described in the box.

Draw lines to match each comment to an organization
that might have made the comment.

Organization	Comment
1 Food Standards Agency	**A** The research did not provide meaningful information. The mice were given undigested aspartame.
2 Representative from a sweeteners information service	**B** The European Union's science committee says that all the additives the scientists used are safe.
3 Food and drink manufacturers	**C** We need more details about the research before we can assess its value. We are also funding research about the effects of combinations of food additives.

[2]

Total [6]

2 Read the article.

Vitamin D cuts cancer risk

US scientists looked in medical journals to find reports on research linking vitamin D levels to cancer rates. They found 63 reports from 1966 to 2004. Each study showed that people who do not have enough vitamin D are more likely to develop certain cancers than people who do have enough vitamin D.

Sunlight helps our bodies to make vitamin D. A glass of milk contains 100 units of vitamin D.

The scientists calculated that taking a vitamin D supplement of 1000 units each day may cut by 50% the risk of getting some cancers. They warn that more than 2000 units of vitamin D each day can damage the liver, bones, and kidneys.

a **i** Underline the sentence that mentions one way in which scientists report their findings to other scientists.

ii Circle the two sentences that show that many scientists collected similar evidence and came to similar conclusions.

iii Draw a box around the paragraph that advises on the daily dose of vitamin D that cuts cancer risks. [3]

b The article claims that a daily vitamin D supplement cuts the risk of getting some cancers.

How strong is the evidence supporting this claim?

Not very

Give one reason for your answer.

because he has not tested it against any organisms. [1]

c In 2015, a scientist collects new evidence about the link between vitamin D and cancer risks. She claims that her evidence shows that vitamin D intake and cancer risks are not related. This contradicts all previous evidence.

Give one reason why other scientists might not want to accept this claim.

Her claims have not been peer assessed. [1]

Total [5]

3 Read the information about the work of Charles Darwin in the1860s.

> Darwin collected evidence by making these observations:
>
> ▶ The individuals of a species are slightly different from each other.
> ▶ There are always more members of a species than can survive.
>
> From his observations, Darwin developed his **theory of natural selection**:
>
> ▶ 'Any variation that helps an individual to survive is more likely to be inherited by its offspring'.
>
> Darwin's theory helps to explain how and why evolution happens.

Below are some statements from other scientists about Darwin's theory. Some statements are from 1870; others are from 2007.

A I don't know why there is variation within a species.

B There has not yet been time for other scientists to evaluate Darwin's ideas.

C DNA evidence explains how species are related to each other.

D I disagree with Darwin's theory. God created everything on Earth in seven days.

E We know that the Earth is about 4 thousand million years old.

F Darwin's observations are fine. But I don't know how living things pass on variations to their offspring.

G We often find new fossils, and we can date them accurately now.

H Darwin's theory has worked well for more than a hundred years.

I There is not enough fossil evidence to support Darwin's ideas.

J The Earth has not existed long enough for evolution to have happened.

K The data may be incorrect.

a Give the letters of four statements that show why many scientists in 1870 did not support Darwin's theory of natural selection.

‾‾‾‾‾

‾‾‾‾‾

‾‾‾‾‾

‾‾‾‾‾ [4]

b Give the letters of three statements that mention **evidence** that might make a 2007 scientist more likely to accept Darwin's theory than an 1870 scientist.

‾‾‾‾‾

‾‾‾‾‾

‾‾‾‾‾ [3]

c In 2020, a scientist collects data that seems to contradict Darwin's theory. He proposes a new explanation for evolution. Most scientists do not immediately accept the new explanation.

Give the letters of two statements that are reasons for scientists not accepting the new explanation.

‾‾‾‾‾

‾‾‾‾‾ [2]

Total [9]

Making decisions about science and technology

1

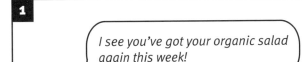

> I see you've got your organic salad again this week!

> Yes. It's delicious. And the farmer uses no synthetic fertilizers or pesticides. So there's no risk of me eating chemicals – like pesticides – that may be harmful.

2

> OK. So people like you – who can afford organic food – benefit. And farmers sell organic food at higher prices than non-organic food. But what about people who need cheaper food?

3

> Exactly. Farmers who use synthetic fertilizers and pesticides get a much higher yield from one square metre of land. So their food is usually cheaper. And there are no bugs in their carrots!

> True. There are always **benefits and costs**. We need to weigh them up. Intensive agriculture can sometimes damage the soil and pollute water.

4

> And organic farming is sustainable?

> I reckon so. **Sustainable development** just means being able to meet people's needs now, and at the same time leaving enough for the future.

> OK. But how do you know your salad really is organic?

> Easy! The Soil Association has checked up on it – they have very strict regulations.

Debating Society: 18 March

Is it ethically acceptable to clone human embryos to produce stem cells to treat illnesses?

1 *I will start with a short explanation. Embryonic stem cells are cells that are not yet specialized; they can develop into any type of cell. To obtain embryonic stem cells, scientists create embryos in the lab. They harvest stem cells from the embryos. Then they destroy what's left of the embryos.*

2 *I believe that that, ethically, the process is totally unacceptable. Life begins at conception. It is wrong and **unnatural** to create and destroy embryos in the lab. I believe this even though I know that stem cell therapy may greatly benefit some people.*

3 *As we have just heard, stem cell therapy has many likely benefits. Stem cells could provide tissue for an organ transplant to save someone's life. They could treat heart disease or diabetes.*

4 *So what do you think, ethically?*

5 *I believe that the right decision is the one that leads to the **best outcome for the majority of people involved**. So if many people will benefit greatly, it is right to go ahead with researching stem cell treatments.*

6 *Even if some people – or embryos – suffer?*

I'm not so sure.

Yes.

163

Making decisions about science and technology

1 Tick the boxes next to the questions that a scientist or technologist could try to answer.

A Should Britain build more nuclear power stations, or concentrate on renewable energy resources instead? ☐

B Could nuclear power meet all Britain's current energy needs? ☐

C What techniques for cloning stem cells are successful? ☐

D Should the MMR vaccination be compulsory? ☐

E Should I buy organic vegetables or those that have been intensively grown? ☐

F How much plastic waste could be recycled in Britain? ☐

G If an AIDS vaccine were available, who should be given it? ☐

H What percentage of children who get the MMR vaccine get ill with measles? ☐

I Is it ethically right to clone stem cells to treat disease? ☐

J Should Britain recycle more of its plastic waste? ☐

K Is it possible to develop an AIDS vaccine? ☐

L How much wheat can be grown in this field using intensive farming techniques? ☐

2 Match each statement to the idea it shows.

Statement	Idea it shows
1 All 11-year-olds should have a flu vaccine. This would protect most of the population from flu, even elderly people who weren't vaccinated themselves.	A It is unfair for some people to have to take the risk so that everyone will benefit.
2 No one should be vaccinated against flu. Vaccinations interfere with nature.	B This decision is the one that benefits the most people.
3 Occasionally, the flu vaccine has side effects. Why should it be only 11-year-olds who are put at risk, when nearly the whole population would benefit?	C Things that are unnatural are never right.

3 Find 12 words from this Ideas about science section in the wordsearch.
Then write a crossword clue for each word.

S	S	N	O	I	T	S	E	U	Q	T
U	N	A	R	T	B	R	I	S	K	E
S	O	B	N	A	E	H	E	R	I	C
T	I	E	E	C	N	Q	S	E	N	H
A	T	V	Y	D	E	U	I	G	S	N
I	A	O	A	N	F	T	E	L	E	I
N	L	L	A	C	I	H	T	E	U	C
A	U	N	N	A	T	U	R	A	L	A
B	G	L	C	O	S	T	S	X	A	L
L	E	L	B	I	S	A	E	F	V	L
E	R	I	M	A	J	O	R	I	T	Y

Word	Clue

4   Read the information in the box about values and ethics in science.
    Then make notes about values and ethics in science in the table.

 ▶   Write a title in the top row.
 ▶   Write the two or three most important points in the next
     row down.
 ▶   Write other, detailed, information in the lowest three rows.

There are many questions that cannot be addressed using a scientific approach. For example, a scientist can find out how to get stem cells from embryos, and how to use the stem cells to treat diseases. But people have different views about whether it is ethically right to actually use these techniques. So it is up to others – not just scientists – to answer the question 'is it ethically acceptable to use embryonic stem cells to treat disease?'

People use different sorts of arguments when they discuss ethical issues. One argument is that the right decision is the one that gives the best outcome for most people. Another argument is that some actions are unnatural or wrong; it is never right to take these actions. Thirdly, some people think that it is unfair for one person to benefit from something when others have taken a risk.

Title:	
Most important points:	
Other information:	

Making decisions about science and technology

1 a An electricity company needs to decide whether to build a new nuclear power station or a coal-fired power station.

The company asks people from five organizations for their opinions.

Freya Electricity from coal and nuclear power stations costs about the same.

Grace Coal-fired power stations lead to acid rain that damages our beautiful buildings.

Hanif Nuclear power stations produce much less carbon dioxide gas than coal-fired power stations.

Ian There is no totally safe way of getting rid of nuclear waste.

Jasmine Nuclear power has its advantages, but an accident at a nuclear power station could kill thousands.

Write the names of the people who would probably prefer the company to build a new coal-fired power station, not a nuclear power station.

_____ [2]

b Old nuclear power stations must be taken down.
This process is called decommissioning.

Tick the boxes next to the jobs that are likely to be part of the work of the Nuclear Decommissioning Authority.

making sure that used fuel rods are disposed of safely ☐

deciding whether to build new nuclear or gas-fired power stations ☐

regularly checking storage sites where low-level and intermediate-level radioactive waste are stored ☐

deciding which countries to buy nuclear fuel from ☐ [2]

Total [4]

2 Pre-implantation genetic screening (PGS) is a technique to choose
the best embryo to implant in a woman who is having fertility treatment.

The technique involves removing one cell from an eight-cell embryo.
Scientists then test this cell for abnormal chromosomes.
Abnormal chromosomes may cause conditions like Down's syndrome.

a Five people were asked for their opinions about PGS.
Some people support the technique; others think it
should not be allowed.

Kirsty

PGS is not natural.

Linda

It is not fair for parents to benefit by putting their embryos at risk – embryos are people too! The parents don't risk much themselves.

It's better to stop babies with genetic defects being born; it's expensive for society to look after them as they grow up.

Marcus

Nikki

People with chromosome abnormalities can have very difficult lives. It's better for them – and their parents – if they are not born in the first place.

People with conditions like Down's syndrome have a lot to offer. It is wrong to prevent them being born.

Oliver

Write the names of the people in the correct columns in the table.

People who *agree* with pre-implantation genetic screening	People who *disagree* with pre-implantation genetic screening

[3]

H

b Write **T** next to the questions that address **technical issues** about PGS.

Write **V** next to the questions that address issues of **values** of PGS.

Is PGS ethically acceptable? ☐

Does the technique damage embryos? ☐

Is it natural to choose which embryo to implant in a woman's uterus? ☐

Do embryos that have been tested grow properly when they are implanted into a woman's uterus? ☐

Is PGS necessary – maybe embryos can fix their own genetic defects? ☐

Is it right to destroy embryos that are not implanted? ☐　　　　[3]

c Suggest two reasons why PGS is offered to parents in the UK but is not offered to parents in some other countries.

_____

_____

_____

_____　　　　[2]

Total [8]

3 Sustainable development is planning how to meet people's needs now without damaging the environment for people in future.

a Tick the boxes next to the statements that show some of the ways in which organic farming is sustainable.

Organic farming does not use synthetic chemical fertilizers that can damage the soil's structure if used carelessly. ☐

Some people think that organic food tastes better. ☐

Organic food is more expensive than food that is not produced on organic farms. ☐

Organic farmers control pests with natural predators, not synthetic pesticides. ☐

Organic food does not have pesticide residues on it. ☐ [2]

b A power station in Bristol burns hospital waste to generate electricity.

i Suggest one way in which generating electricity from hospital waste is more sustainable than simply burning hospital waste.

_____

_____ [1]

ii It is technically possible to use waste from all British hospitals to generate electricity.

However, waste from only a few hospitals is used in this way.

Suggest two reasons for this.

_____

_____

_____

_____ [2]

Total [5]

H 4 **a** Malaria kills millions of people every year.
There is no vaccine against malaria.
Below are some reasons for this.

Malaria parasites become resistant to new drugs and vaccines very quickly. ☐

Malaria mainly affects people living in economically poor countries. ☐

There are several different malaria parasites. Each needs a different vaccine. ☐

Drug companies make more money from selling drugs for heart disease than they could make from a malaria vaccine. ☐

Governments of economically rich countries are unwilling to spend money on scientific research to develop a malaria vaccine. ☐

Write **T** next to the statements that give **technical** reasons for there being no malaria vaccine.

Write **V** next to the statements that give **values-related** reasons for there being no malaria vaccine. [3]

b All British babies are offered the MMR vaccine against measles, mumps, and rubella.
Some parents decide not to have their babies vaccinated.

i Give one reason why some people think that parents should be free to choose whether or not their baby gets the MMR vaccine.

_____

_____

_____ [1]

ii Give one reason why some people think that the MMR vaccine should be compulsory.

_____

_____

_____ [1]

Total [5]

Case study

The case study is your chance to find out more about a science-related issue that interests **you**. It's worth 20% of your total mark.

Choosing a topic

You need to find a science topic that is controversial – one that people have different opinions about. To get ideas, look in newspapers and magazines, or pick things up from television, radio, or the Internet.

It's best to choose from one of the topic types in the table.

Topic type	Examples	What to focus on
evaluating a claim where scientific knowledge is uncertain	▶ Is there life elsewhere in the Universe? ▶ Does using mobile phones increase risk of brain damage?	▶ relationships between data and explanations ▶ the quality of research behind different scientists' claims
helping to make a decision on a science-related issue	▶ Should a shopping street be pedestrianized to reduce air pollution? ▶ Should pre-implantation genetic screening be available free to anyone who wants to have a baby? ▶ Should Britain build new nuclear power stations?	▶ personal choice and values ▶ balancing risks and benefits of possible action
personal or social choices	▶ Should my child receive the MMR vaccine? ▶ Should I recycle all the plastic I use?	▶ personal and ethical issues ▶ using science to evaluate these issues

For the title, make up a question that you can answer by balancing evidence and opinions.

Selecting and using information (4 marks)

▶ Choose sources of information that are
  – varied, for example books, leaflets, newspaper articles, and websites
  – reliable: research reports from a university website may be more reliable than an individual's blog; journalists have their own opinions and don't always give balanced views; an organization that pays for a piece of science research may influence the research findings
  – relevant: if something is not relevant, throw it out!
▶ At the end of your report, include references to every source. Make it easy for someone else to find the information you have used (and check up on you!).
▶ Throughout your report, give the exact source of every quotation and opinion.

The science of the case (8 marks)

- Check what the scientific knowledge you need in order to understand the issues in your study. You should be able to find most of it either in your Textbook or in another source written at a similar level.
- Consider how well (or badly!) each opinion that you describe is supported by a science explanation.
- Look carefully at the quality of scientific evidence in each source to judge whether its claims are reliable.

In your report, you need to show that you've done all this – doing it but not writing about it counts for nothing! So include plenty of detail, and make sure that you link every claim or opinion to relevant scientific evidence.

If the science is too difficult, it is best to choose another topic.

Your conclusions (8 marks)

This is another chance to show how well you've understood Ideas about science, particularly: data and their limitations; risk; making decisions.

In your conclusion

- Compare opposing evidence and views.
  - Report and evaluate arguments 'for' and 'against'
  - Compare these arguments carefully and critically
- Give conclusions and recommendations.
  - Suggest two or three different conclusions to show you realize that evidence can be interpreted in different ways.

Presenting your report (4 marks)

First of all, decide on an 'audience' for your report – this could be Year 9 students, a Member of Parliament, or any other individual or group.

Depending on the resources available, you might produce a formal written report, a newspaper article, a poster, or a PowerPoint presentation. Think about what is most appropriate for your audience and what you want to tell them. Whatever method you use, make sure that it looks attractive!

Then work on the following:

- The structure and organization of your report:
  - Put everything in a logical order, with plenty of subheadings.
  - Include page numbers and a contents list.
- Visual communication:
  - Include pictures, diagrams, charts, or tables to help your audience understand ideas and information.
- Spelling, punctuation and grammar
  - Be concise – don't waste words!
  - Use relevant scientific words.
  - Check your spelling, punctuation, and grammar very carefully.

Data analysis

This is your chance to have a go at interpreting and analysing real data. It's worth 13.3% of your total mark.

Getting started

Start by doing a practical activity to collect the data you need. You can do this on your own or in a small group. Once you've collected some data yourself, you may be able to get the rest from other students, a teacher demonstration, or other sources.

Interpreting data

Follow the advice below, and you should get a high mark!

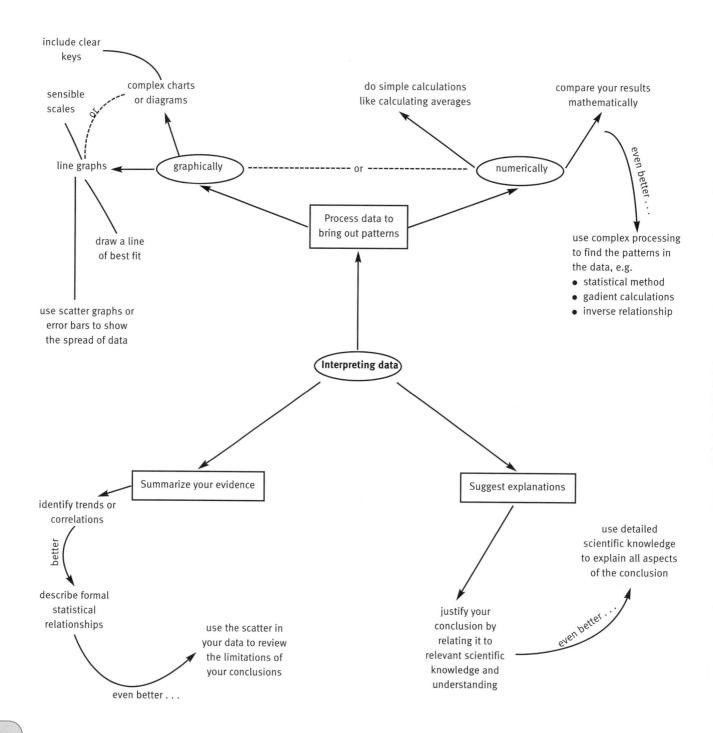

Evaluating data

Follow the advice below to achieve the very best you can!

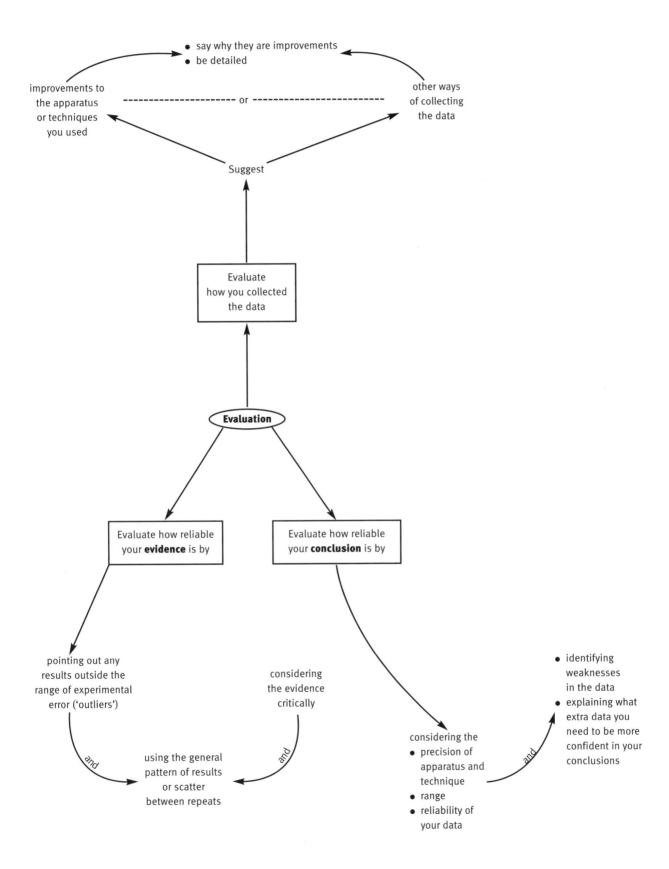

Investigation

Your practical investigation counts for 33.3 % of your total grade. You will do the work in class. If you do more than one investigation, your teacher will choose the best one for your marks.

What you will do

In your investigation you will:

▶ choose a question to investigate
▶ select equipment and use it safely and appropriately
▶ make accurate and reliable observations

How your teacher will award marks

Your teacher will award marks under five headings.

Strategy

▶ Choose the task for your investigation.
▶ Decide how much data to collect.
▶ Choose equipment and techniques to give you precise and reliable data.

To get high marks here, choose a task which is not too simple. Plan to collect an appropriate range of precise and reliable data. Give reasons for your choice of equipment and techniques. Try to work as independently as possible.

Collecting data

▶ Work safely.
▶ Take careful and accurate measurements.
▶ Collect enough data and repeat it to check its reliability.
▶ Collect data across an appropriate range.
▶ Control other things that might affect your results.

To get high marks here, do preliminary work to decide the range. Collect data across the whole range. Repeat readings to make them as reliable as possible. Make sensible decisions about how to treat anomalous results (outliers). Use the apparatus skilfully to make precise readings. Try changing your techniques if you think that might give you better data.

Interpreting data

▶ Use charts, tables, diagrams, or graphs to show patterns in your results.
▶ Say what conclusions you can make from your data.
▶ Explain your conclusions using your science knowledge and understanding.

To get high marks here, label graph axes and table headings correctly. If appropriate, analyse your results mathematically. Summarize your evidence by identifying trends and correlations. Say whether there are any limitations in your data. Finally, use detailed scientific knowledge to explain your conclusion.

Evaluation

▶ Look back at your experiment and say how you could improve the method.
▶ Say how reliable you think your evidence is.
▶ Suggest improvements or extra data you could collect to be more confident in your conclusions.

To get high marks here, describe improvements to the method in detail. Say why they would be improvements. Use the pattern of your results, and the scatter between repeats, to help you to assess accuracy and reliability. Give reasons for any anomalous results. Say how confident you are in your conclusions, and give reasons for your decision. Describe in detail what extra data you would like to collect to make your conclusions more secure.

Presentation

▶ Write a full report of your investigation.
▶ Choose a sensible order for the different parts of your report, and lay it out clearly.
▶ Describe the apparatus you used and what you did with it.
▶ Show units correctly.
▶ Make sure your spelling, punctuation and grammar are accurate.
▶ Use scientific words when appropriate.

To get high marks here, state your investigation question clearly. Describe accurately and in detail how you did the practical work. Include all the data you collected, including repeat values. Make sure you record the data with appropriate accuracy and that you include all units. Record all your observations thoroughly and in detail.

Secondary data

As well as the data you collect, you may also use information from other people's work. This is secondary data. You can get secondary data from other students, the Internet, libraries, and textbooks. Or you might like to speak to a scientist or write to an organization. Think carefully about what you want to find out before looking for secondary data. This will help you to get the information you need without wasting time!

Answers to questions

B1 Workout

1 **a** Cell **b** Genes   **c** Nucleus
   d Chromosome   **e** DNA

2 **a** T **b** T **c** F **d** F
   e F **f** T **g** F **h** T

3 Unspecialized, asexual, clones, environments

4 1J, 2N, 3A, 4D, 5G, 6H, 7I or B or F or L, 8B or F or L or I,
   9E or P, 10M, 11B or F or L, 12C, 13O, 14B or F or L, 15P
   or E, 16K

B1 GCSE-style questions

1 **a** They have the same combination of alleles. They both
       developed from one egg that was fertilized by one sperm.
       They both started growing from one embryo. The cells of
       the embryo separated.
   b A person's characteristics are affected by both genes
       and the environment. They received alleles from both
       parents. The twins and their mother have different
       combinations of alleles.
   c XX
   d They have different lifestyles.

2 Chromosomes; information; proteins;
   characteristic

3 Unspecialized; embryos; research

4 **a i** 50%   **ii** 2
   b i   **ii** 50%

   c Any one of height, eye colour, skin colour, or many
       other possible characteristics.

5 **a** Loss of control over movements; memory loss and
       mental deterioration
   b Abigail and Brenda
   c i His employer may not want him to work for
         the company for long; he may miss out on
         promotion.
     ii Advantage: they can consider having a
         termination if the test is positive. Disadvantage:
         deciding whether or not to have a termination is a
         very difficult decision.

B2 Workout

1 Sweat, skin, tears, stomach acid

2 Top empty box: reproduce rapidly
   Empty boxes on middle line: make toxins *and*
   reproduce rapidly Bottom empty box: disease
   symptoms

3 C E F B D

4 **a** Experts meet in April...
   b The eggs provide food...
   c In October...
   d This flu virus is delivered...

5 **a** T **b** T **c** T **d** T **e** F

6 **a**

Part of circulation system	What does it do?	What is it made from?
heart	It pumps blood around your body.	muscle
artery	It takes blood from your heart to the rest of your body.	Arteries are tubes. They have thick walls made of muscle and elastic fibres.
vein	It brings blood back to your heart from the rest of your body.	Veins are tubes. They have thin walls made of muscle and elastic fibres.

   b i If fat builds up inside the coronary arteries, a
         blood clot may form on the fatty lump. If the clot
         blocks an artery, part of the heart muscle does not
         get oxygen. The cells start to die and the heart is
         permanently damaged.
     ii Any three from: cut down on fatty foods; stop
         smoking; lose weight if you are overweight; take
         regular exercise; eat less salt; if necessary, take
         drugs to reduce blood pressure and cholesterol
         level.

B2 GCSE-style questions

1 **a** The cough was caused by a virus.
   b i They killed the bacteria that caused the painful
         ear.
     ii Random changes (mutations) in bacteria make
         new varieties that are less affected by antibiotics.
         Some of these varieties survive a course of
         antibiotics. Not finishing the course increases the
         likelihood of bacteria becoming resistant to
         antibiotics.

2 **a** Smoking cigarettes; drinking too much alcohol; not
       taking regular exercise
   b The heart needs a continuous supply of energy; blood
       brings a constant supply of glucose and oxygen to the
       heart.
   c E D A C

3 **a** Stomach acid
   b i Reproduction
     ii 4
   c i White
     ii Taking anti-diarrhoea tablets would mean that
         Salmonella bacteria would stay in the intestines for
         longer.
   d Resistant; killed; bacteria

4 **a** Increased; opinion B *or* C *or* D
       Decreased; opinion A
   b E C B D
   c To protect everyone from the disease – even those who
       cannot be vaccinated for some reason

B3 Workout

1 Natural selection only: C, E
   Selective breeding only: B
   Both: A, D

2 **a** Effector cells
b Neuron
c Central nervous system
d Neuron
e Receptor cells

5

N	T	S	Y	S	T	E	M
E	H	U	Y	E	R	S	A
U	R	R	P	X	A	P	N
R	E	V	O	L	V	E	D
O	E	I	C	O	E	C	D
N	E	V	E	R	L	I	O
S	E	A	R	T	H	E	O
S	O	L	A	R	C	S	F

B3 GCSE-style questions

1 **a** Electrical; brain; chemicals; slowly; long
b Nervous system changes – A, B, F; hormone system changes – C, D, E

2 **a** Studying fossils; analysing the DNA of modern cats, lions, and other species of the cat family
b **i** Selection
ii B, D, A
c **i** 6.7 million years ago
ii Fishing cat
iii Environmental; mutations; selection

3 **a** Global warming
b **i** Antarctic whelk *or* brittlestar *or Trematomus bernacchii* fish
ii Their populations will decrease.
c Environmental conditions change; another living thing in the brittlestar's food chain becomes extinct.

B4 Workout

1 Vigorous exercise – temperature, hydration, salt levels, blood oxygen levels; mountain climbing – blood oxygen levels; living in hot climates – temperature, hydration, salt levels; scuba-diving – blood oxygen levels

2 Receptor – to detect stimuli – temperature sensor; processing centre – to receive information and coordinate responses – thermostat with switch; effector – to produce the response – heater

3 Protein, speed up, 37, slow, there are few collisions between enzyme molecules and reacting molecules, denatured, the shape of the active site changes, active site, lock and key

4 1F, 2C, 3G, 4B, 5F, 6A, 7D, 8E

5 **2** Hot dry skin, fast pulse rate, dizzy and confused
3 42
4 When it is very hot you sweat more. This made you dehydrated. So you sweated less. So your body temperature rose out of control and your body's normal methods of temperature control stopped working.

6 **2** Shivering, confusion, slurred speech, not co-ordinated
3 Insulate him, warm him slowly with warm towels, give him a warm drink

4 35 °C. His body lost energy faster than it gained energy.

7 **a** DO **b** DO **c** D **d** D **e** DO
f D **g** O **h** A **i** A

8 **a** Enters in food, drinks and as a result of respiration; leaves in sweating, breathing, faeces, urine
b **i** ... the membrane may rupture
ii ... solutions in the cell get too concentrated so the cell cannot work properly

9 C E A D B

10 **a** T **b** T **c** T **d** T **e** F
f F **g** F **h** T **i** T **j** F
k F

11 1 A, 2 C, 3 D, 4 K, 5 E, 6 F, 7 B, 8 G, 9 H, 10 L, 11 I, 12 J

B4 GCSE-style questions

1 **a** Temperature sensor – skin; heater (switched on) – muscle cells (contracting quickly to cause shivering); thermostat with a switch – brain; heater (switched off) – sweat glands
b **i** If there is a change in the system, there is an action that reverses the change.
ii e.g. The response is very sensitive.

2 **a** Protein
b **i** At 30 °C collisions between catalase and hydrogen peroxide are more frequent and have more energy.
ii It has been denatured.
c A
d **i** Active site
ii The shape of the active site is changed so reacting molecules no longer fit into the active site.

3 **a** Two from: hot dry skin, fast pulse rate, dizzy, confused
b Sensors
c You are less likely to get dehydrated so you can continue to sweat.
d The brain and other organs return to normal temperature.
e When sweat evaporates, energy is transferred from skin to sweat. This cools you down. If you do not sweat, your body's temperature rises out of control.
f **i** Processing centre
ii Alcohol results in big volumes of dilute urine, so less water is available to make sweat.
g The body detects that it is losing too much heat. So it shuts down circulation to the skin. So all the hot blood in the skin is diverted towards the brain.

4 **a** Two from: water, carbon dioxide, oxygen
b **i** Molecules move from a region of their high concentration to a region of their low concentration through a partially permeable membrane.
ii The cell may rupture.
c Na^+ ion – diffusion; K^+ ion – active transport; water molecule – osmosis

B5 Workout

1 Chromosomes, genes, DNA, double helix, copied

2 Top row: A, D, H; bottom row: 1B, 2G, 3F, 4C, 5E

3 **1** testes, meiosis, 4, sperm; **2** 23; **3** ovaries, meiosis, 4, eggs; **4** 23; **5** fertilization; **6** zygote, 23, 46; **7** mitosis, 2, 46; **8** 2, 4; **9** 4, 8; **10** stem; **11** 16

4

	Meiosis	Mitosis
What does it make?	gametes (sex cells)	body cells
How many new cells does each parent cell make?	4	2
How many chromosomes are in each new cell?	half as many as in the parent cell	same as in parent cell
Where does it happen?	in sex organs	in body cells
Why does it happen?	to make sex cells for sexual reproduction	so an organism can grow, reproduce and replace damaged cells

5 Correct bold words: **a** weak, 2; **b** T, C; **c** 4; **d** 2
Matching pairs: 1**c**, 2**a**, 3**b**, 4**d**

6 For example:
1 Treating disease and replacing damaged tissues, for example growing skin cell to treat burns and growing nerve cells to treat spinal injuries.
3 All their genes are still switched on – they can grow into any type of specialized cell.
4 Patients must take drugs to stop their bodies rejecting the transplanted tissue.
5 The genes of the new tissues are the same as the patient's.
6 The genes are different to the patient's.
7 Treat burns and spinal injuries.

7 Plants – A, C, G, I; animals – D, F; both – B, E, H

8 —

9 Auxin, chromosomes, double, embryonic, fetus, gametes, mitochondria, nucleus, organelles, phototropism, tissues, unspecialized, xylem, young, zygote

B5 GCSE-style questions

1 **a** Gametes, testes, 4, different, 15
b **i** Egg or ovum
ii Fertilization
c C A D B

2 **a** **i** They can grow many plants quickly and cheaply; they can reproduce a plant with exactly the features they want.
ii Auxins
iii Meristem cells
iv Leaves, flowers
b **i** Plants need light energy for photosynthesis – the more light that falls on the leaf, the faster photosynthesis happens (up to a maximum speed).
ii Phototropism
iii B

3 **a** **i** Stem cells are unspecialized cells. They divide and develop into specialized cells.
ii They will grow heart muscle cells from the stem cells.
b **i** One of: embryos, adults
ii One of: (embryos) ethical objections, problem of rejection; (adults) difficult to separate from other cells, problem of rejection

4 **a** Double helix
b It gives instruction for joining amino acids in the correct order to make a certain protein.
c B A D C

B6 Workout

1 Stimulus, response, behaviour

2 **a** Grasping a finger or similar tightly in palm
b Sucking nipple in mouth
c Stepping when feet touch flat surface
d Startling (or Moro reflex) - spreading out arms and legs on hearing a loud noise

3 **a** S **b** C **c** S **d** S **e** C

4 Receptors: A B E F; effectors: C D G H

5 Left from top: motor neuron, sensory neuron, effector, receptor
Right: spinal cord

6 A F C D E B

7 Nucleus – controls cell; cytoplasm – cell reactions happen here; cell membrane – substances get into and out of the cell through this; fatty sheath – insulates neuron from neighbouring cells; branched endings – make connections with other neurons or effectors.

8 Bird: Those caterpillars are poisonous. She won't eat them again because they taste so bad.
Caterpillar: She's learnt that caterpillars like us don't taste good – so that's one less bird that's going to try to eat me.

9 From the top: The sensory neuron releases a chemical into the synapse and the chemical diffuses across the synapse; a nerve impulse gets to the end of the sensory neuron; the chemical arrives at receptor molecules on the motor neuron's membrane and the chemical's molecules bind to the receptor molecules. This stimulates a nerve impulse in the motor neuron.

10 Short-term memory A C; long-term memory B, D; both E

11 **a** Consciousness, language, intelligence, memory
b … studying patients with brain damage, electrically stimulating different parts of the brain, doing MRI scans.
c … adapt to new situations and learn to interact effectively with others.
d Neurons, pathways

12 A F C E B D G H

13 Horizontal: 3 consciousness, 5 multi-store, 6 repetition, 7 shop, 8 muscle, 9 feral, 10 axon, 11 CNS, 12 cortex, 13 N, 14 pathways, 15 short-term, 16 model, 17 neuroscientist
Vertical: 1 serotonin, 2 synapse, 3 cerebral, 4 neuron, 15 stimulus

B6 GCSE-style questions

1 a Grips finger; spreads out arms and legs when she hears a sudden noise.
   b . . . something being put in her mouth; milk
   c e.g. Cannot respond to new situations, so often fail to survive environmental changes

2 a Effector cells – make changes in response to stimulus; receptor cells – detect a stimulus; brain and spinal cord – control the body's response to a stimulus
   b i (Left) sensory neuron, (right top) central nervous system), (right bottom) motor neuron
   ii Electrical, peripheral, central

3 a A dolphin's brain has a great variety of potential neuron pathways.

   b A C E D B F G

4 a Stimulus, response, learned, conditioned
   b i The bitter taste means the insect may be poisonous. So the bird has avoided eating something poisonous.
   ii Birds do not eat hover flies because they look as though they might have a bitter taste and therefore be poisonous.

5 a A C E B F D
   b Ecstasy causes an increase in the concentration of serotonin in the brain; Ecstasy blocks sites in the brain's synapses where serotonin is removed.

B7.1 Workout

1 a light with the wrong wavelength for photosynthesis 60%

   transferred to organic materials 2%

   transferred as waste heat 33%

   passes straight through 5%

   b 2%

2

decomposers	micro-organisms that feed on and decay dead organisms
autotrophs	organisms which produce their own organic compounds
consumers	organisms that eats others
heterotrophs	organisms that obtain organic compounds by eating other organisms
producers	organisms that are able to make their own food; they are the autotrophs at the start of food chains
carnivores	animals that feed on other animals
herbivores	animals that feed on plants; they are primary consumers

3 a 1 matches C   2 matches B   3 matches A
   b A pyramid of **biomass** for an ecosystem shows the mass of the organisms at each **tropic/feeding** level. It shows how much **biomass/mass** passes from one level to the next.

4 a tertiary consumer   the Sun   secondary consumer   primary consumer   producer

b The **producers** in this ecosystem transformed 10 000 of 1 000 000 units of energy into biomass. 800 of these units were transferred to **primary** consumers.
   c i 800/10 000 × 100 = 8%
   ii 160/800 × 100 = 20%

B7.1 GCSE-style questions

1 a A cabbage   B cat   C cabbage
   b Start at cabbage and end at cat, for example cabbage-> aphid -> blue tit -> cat
   c When one organism **eats** another, only about 10 percent of the **energy** is transferred to the organism. This is because some of the energy is transferred in life processes such as **moving** and keeping **warm**, and some is transferred to the surroundings as **heat**. Also, some energy remains in undigested **waste**. In the same way, when decomposers feed on **dead** organisms and waste **materials**, only part of the energy is transferred.

2 a The Sun
   b producers/autotrophs
   c carbohydrates/starch/fats/oils
   d arrow points upwards
   e Sharks because are the top level and there is less mass and energy at each level as you go up a pyramid.
   f 28/200 = 14%

3 a

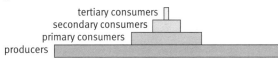

   b

   c The first pyramid is based on a large number of small producers. The second is based on one large producer.
   d Showing the mass at each level, both pyramids would then be pyramid-shaped. However, they would have to collect more data to find the mass of the organisms at each level.
   e

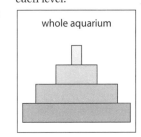 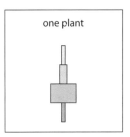

4 a air
   b i Biomass lost is mass lost from dry soil = 20 − 18 = 2g
   % biomass in the original mass of the soil = $\frac{2}{25}$ × 100 = 8%
   ii Mass of soil at end of experiment = 18g
   % of original soil remaining = $\frac{18}{25}$ × 100 = 72%

Answers

B7.2 Workout

1

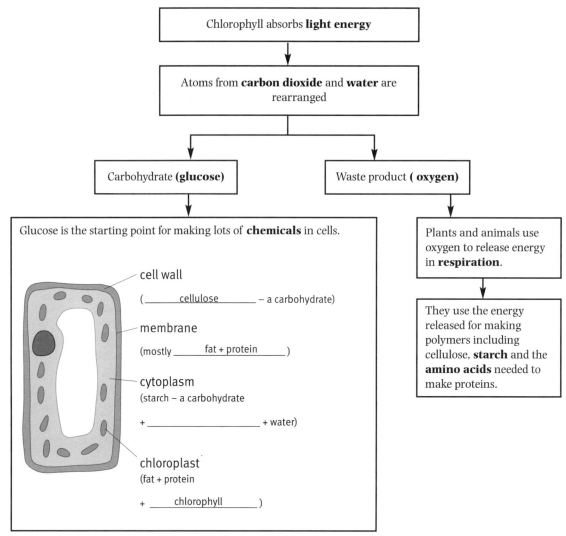

2 **a** True **b** True **c** False **d** True **e** False **f** True **g** False

B7.2 GCSE-style questions

1 **a** Respiration
   b Their pieces of pond weed varied. The distance between their plants and the light was not exactly the same. They didn't all count/time accurately. Other sensible suggestion.
   c Add all their results and calculate the average number of bubbles.
   d To allow for the variability of their pond weed and any variables in their procedure.

2 **a** Photosynthesis is increasing at the highest rate. **A** Carbon dioxide is limiting the rate of photosynthesis. **B** Extra carbon dioxide has increased the rate of photosynthesis. **C**
   b Temperature.

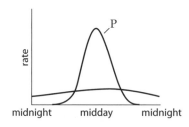

3 **a** Line P. This process, like photosynthesis, is happening during daylight hours only.
   b Where lines cross.
   c Movement of carbon dioxide in the plant is equal to movement out.

4 **a** − 6 to 2 °C; 8 °C
   b That it has varied.

c No. Although the trend is upwards, the graph shows that the temperature in the Antarctic has been both higher and lower than it is at present. Global warming is a rise in the average temperature of the Earth. This data is for the Antarctic only. Any trends may not be representative of global trends.

d There is a match between the pattern of the variation in temperature and the variation in concentration of greenhouse gases in the atmosphere.

e The graphs show the changes but not the causes of the changes. There could be other causes such as the amount of volcanic activity.

B7.3 Workout

1

Definition	Type of association	Example
A relationship between two organisms of different species which benefits one but neither harms nor benefits the other.	**commensalism**	Seeds in hooked burrs spread or dispersed on animal fur.
An association between two organisms of different species which is beneficial to both.	**symbiosis**	Cellulose-digesting bacteria in the guts of cattle.
A close association between two organisms of different species which benefits one and harms the other.	**parasitism**	The protozoan that causes malaria.

2 "I've got malaria. A parasite in my **blood** is making me very ill. Malaria is spread by **mosquitoes**."

"I've got threadworms. I eat enough but I'm very thin. I'm suffering from **malnutrition** because the worms use my **food**."

"Root eelworms are damaging my crops so the **yield** is low and I haven't enough **food** for my family."

"My cows have parasites that use some of the cows' **food**. So the cows produce **less** milk."

3 A faulty recessive allele.

4

My problem	My solution
Contractions of the gut wall try to push me out.	I have hooks and suckers to hold onto the gut wall.
Digestive enzymes in the gut could harm me.	I have a thick cuticle to resist enzymes.
There's little or no oxygen inside the gut.	I can respire anaerobically.
I live on my own so I haven't a mate.	I have male and female sex organs so I can reproduce without a mate.
I can produce eggs on my own, but the chances of them finding the next host are small.	I produce lots of eggs to increase the chances.

5 1 Adult tapeworm in the gut.
4 Egg hatches in a pig's muscle.
6 Tapeworm develops in human intestine.
3 Eggs eaten by a pig.
2 Eggs released into faeces.
5 Human eats undercooked pork.

B7.3 GCSE-style questions

1 a A close association between two organisms of different species that benefits the parasite but harms the host.

b threadworms in human guts √
ivy growing on a tree √
(nitrogen-fixing bacteria in the root nodules of legumes)
(clown fish in a giant anemone)

c Because they live inside red blood cells, they are protected against the immune system for much of the time. They have different surface markers at different stages in their life cycle so it is harder for white blood cells to recognise them.

d Human diseases. Reduced yields of food crops. Slowed growth of farm animals.

2 Symbiosis; one organism benefits and the other is harmed. Many correct examples are possible.

3 C, A, D, B, E, G, F

4 a X.
b Blood vessels get blocked when cells 'sickle'/severe anaemia.
c W and Z.
d The frequency of the sickle-cell allele is generally higher in the areas where there is malaria than in areas where malaria is absent.
e Having one copy of the sickle-cell allele gives some protection against malaria. People who live in a malaria area and have one copy of the allele are more likely to survive than those without the allele. They pass on the allele to the next generation. So the frequency of the allele remains higher than it does in non-malaria areas.
f Natural selection.

B7.4 Workout

1 C

2

					¹g	e	n	e		
					²e	n	z	y	m	e
				³d	n	a				
			⁴a	l	l	e	l	e		
⁵f	e	r	m	e	n	t	e	r		
	⁶i	n	s	u	l	i	n			
		⁷n	u	c	l	e	u	s		

Your clue: Genetic - to do with genes.

Answers

3

Example of genetically modified organism (GMO)	Benefit
F 1. Scientists transferred the <u>human insulin gene</u> to bacteria. These bacteria, grown in a fermenter, produce human insulin.	Diabetics can use human insulin made by bacteria instead of using animal insulin.
F 2. Genetically modified yeast produces the rennet we use for making vegetarian cheese.	Rennet from calves' stomachs is no longer essential for cheese-making.
Y 3. A gene for (herbicide resistance) from a bacterium was transferred into sugar beet.	This GM sugar beet is not killed by the weed-killer 'Roundup'.
4. Scientists cancelled out the gene for an enzyme that makes tomatoes soften as they ripen.	This made the fruit more resistant to rot so they keep for longer.
5. A gene for increasing vitamin A production was added to rice. The modified rice is called 'Golden Rice'.	This can reduce the vitamin A deficiency that causes eyesight problems, including blindness.
Y 6. A gene for a pesticide was transferred from a bacterium into corn.	This reduces damage by the insects that feed on corn. Yields increase.

4 Eureka! We've found the **gene** that allows the bacterium to make this chemical!
We can use an enzyme to cut the gene out and a **different** enzyme to copy it.
Then we'll put copies of the gene into sugar beet cell **nuclei**.*
We can grow the sugar beet cells with the new gene into new **plants**.
The new gene works! Our plants are making the **chemical** that kills **insect** pests.

* **Higher tier** using a vector

5

Use gentle heat to separate the two strands of the DNA.	5
Use enzymes to cut up the DNA.	4
Produce a gene probe for the allele.	1
Use UV or autoradiography to locate gene probe.	7
Extract DNA from white blood cells.	3
Take a blood sample and separate out the white blood cells.	2
Add the gene probe to the DNA fragments.	6

Sally is the carrier - the matching gene is ATCTG.

B7.4 GCSE-style questions

1 a Bacteria and yeasts.
b Two from antibiotics, enzymes, alcohol, single-cell protein.
2 Any example such as, **a** bacteria, **b** human, **c** so the bacteria make human insulin to treat diabetes in humans.
3 a Making copies.
b An enzyme catalyses only one reaction,

4 a To carry a new gene into a cell.
b Viruses and bacteria.
5 a i Single.   ii UV light or X-ray film.
b For example, DNA fingerprinting/genetic testing.
c They extract DNA from cells and use enzymes to chop it into pieces. They then heat the pieces to separate the two strands and add gene probes. If the gene is present, the gene probe sticks to it and is detected.
6 a i Environmentalist/developing world charity worker or similar.
   ii Researcher or manager in a company involved in GM
b We use fewer pesticides when we grow plants that produce their own pesticides.
c i They may be allergic to nuts.
   ii They may be vegan.
   iii Religious reasons.
d Any sensible idea. Expensive GM seed makes it even harder for people in the developing world to make a living. The risk of contaminating the environment is too great. We shouldn't transfer genes from animals such as pigs into food crops as some people have a religious objection to eating them.
e i Pollen from GM crops may pollinate related wild plants or nearby non-GM plants spreading the added gene throughout the environment.
   ii The precautionary principle is that if an action or policy might cause harm, that action should not be taken. It is up to anyone proposing such an action to prove that it will do no harm.

B7.5 Workout

1 Figure: To contract, **muscles** need energy from respiration.

Your cells need **oxygen** for respiration. You get oxygen from the **air** that you breathe into your **lungs**. You breathe more **quickly** when you exercise.

Your heart pumps **blood** containing oxygen to your tissues. When you exercise your heart beats more **quickly**.

Sometimes the amount of **oxygen** reaching the muscles is too low. Then the muscle **cells** use **anaerobic** respiration. The waste product **lactic** acid builds up in the **muscles**.

Caption: During exercise cells respire **faster** to provide additional **energy** for movement.

Word equation blanks are **energy, equation, glucose**

Aerobic respiration releases more energy from a glucose molecule than **anaerobic** respiration. However, when cells are short of oxygen, anaerobic respiration is of benefit to humans and other **organisms**. Humans need **oxygen** to break down the lactic acid in muscle cells. The amount needed is called the **oxygen** debt. The breakdown of the lactic acid releases more **energy**.

2 Rings around aerobic, a product, out of, fat, energy currency

H 3

¹B	R	E	A	T	**H**			
		²E	X	E	**R**	C	I	S	E
			³A	I	**R**		
⁴R	E	S	P	I	**R**	E	
	⁴C	O	N	**T**	R	A	C	T

Your clue: The organ that pumps blood around the body.

B7.5 GCSE-style questions

1 **a** glucose + oxygen ⟶ carbon dioxide + water (+ energy released)
   b Glucose is the fuel/a reactant energy is released.
   c Oxygen is a reactant in aerobic but not in anaerobic respiration. More energy is released in aerobic than in anaerobic respiration.
   d In cells.

2 **a** The rates of heartbeat and breathing increase.
   b Muscles contract

3 The graph shows Donna's rate of oxygen uptake during and after exercise.
   a Need to know which alternative you used here.
   b **i** The oxygen debt.
      ii To break down the lactic acid that has accumulated in Donna's cells and release the energy from it.
   c ATP.
   d Respiration.

4 **a** 58-90 or 32 beats per minute
   b Variation in heart rate varies according to fitness and other factors.
   c 73.4 beats per minute.
   d On average, heart rate increases with exercise.
   e **i** An anomalous result. **ii** Col measured his pulse rate incorrectly or wrote it down incorrectly.
   f Pete. There was a very small increase in his pulse rate that suggests possible stress rather than exercise. Col's result is more likely to be a mistake.

B7.6 Workout

1

Component	What it is	Its function
A	Red blood cell	To transport oxygen.
B	White blood cell	To fight infection/destroy bacteria.
C	Platelet	To help to clot blood.

2 Antigens/~~antibodies~~ are markers on the surface of foreign cells; including the surface of **red/~~white~~** blood cells. ~~Antigens~~/**antibodies** are substances in blood plasma. They are made by ~~red~~/**white** blood cells and they destroy foreign cells.

3

Blood type	Antigens	Antibodies
A	A	Anti-b
B	B	Anti-a
AB	A and B	none
O	neither	Anti-a+b

Blood type **AB**. They have neither Anti-a nor Anti-B in their blood so they can receive blood from anyone without risk of 'clotting'.

4 **a** False **b** True **c** False **d** False **e** True **f** False

5 **a**

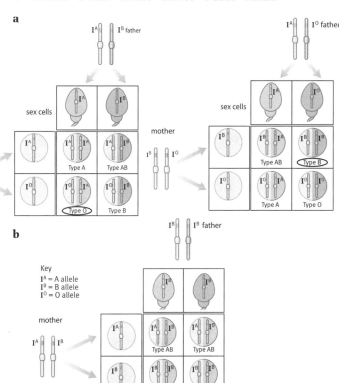

b

Answers

6 a

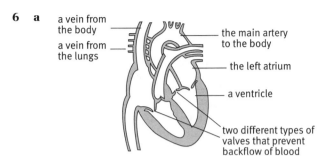

- a vein from the body
- a vein from the lungs
- the main artery to the body
- the left atrium
- a ventricle
- two different types of valves that prevent backflow of blood

b

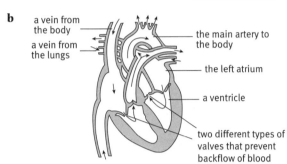

- a vein from the body
- a vein from the lungs
- the main artery to the body
- the left atrium
- a ventricle
- two different types of valves that prevent backflow of blood

7 **a** Exchanges between your blood and your cells happen in **capillary** networks. The walls of these blood vessels are only **one** cell thick. Water and **dissolved** substances are squeezed out of these vessels as a result of high blood **pressure**. The concentration of substances such as oxygen and **glucose** is lower in the cells than in this fluid. So they **pass** into the cells. Two waste products that pass from the cells into the blood are **carbon dioxide** and **urea**.

b

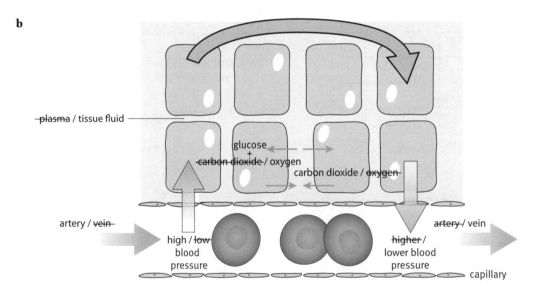

- ~~plasma~~ / tissue fluid
- glucose + ~~carbon dioxide~~ / oxygen
- carbon dioxide / ~~oxygen~~
- artery / ~~vein~~
- high / ~~low~~ blood pressure
- ~~higher~~ / lower blood pressure
- ~~artery~~ / vein
- capillary

2 a i 1 **ii** O **iii** They are both dominant so when they are both present, they both show up.

b

		A	A
		B	AB Type AB
AB Type AB		O	AO Type A

3 a In one circulation around the body, the blood flows through your heart twice. It flows alternately through the lungs then around the rest of the body. The blood that goes to the lungs has just been around the body and given up its oxygen; it is deoxygenated.

b Red blood cell.

c i The left ventricle wall needs to be thicker, so more muscular to pump blood around the body. The right ventricle wall is thinner, with less muscle as it pumps blood only to the lungs.

ii Blood in veins is returning to the heart from the tissues. So there is less pressure to keep the blood flowing. Valves prevent blood from flowing the wrong way / backflow.

iii When the ventricles stop contracting, blood could flow back into them. The valves prevent backflow of blood into the ventricles.

iv Arteries have to withstand the pressure of blood pumped by the heart. The pressure would be lost if

B7.6 GCSE-style questions

1 a A, B, AB and O

b The red blood cells clump together, they block blood vessels and the person dies.

c

Recipient Donor	O anti-A + anti-B	A anti-B	B anti-A	AB none
O anti-A + anti-B	—	—	—	—
A anti-B	🔴	—	🔴	—
B anti-A	🔴	🔴	—	—
AB none	🔴	🔴	🔴	—

Key
— no clotting
 clotting

the artery walls were too thin and stretchy. The blood in veins is under low pressure so the walls can be thinner.

v Capillaries are important for the exchange of materials between the blood and tissues. Their walls are only one cell thick, so blood pressure can force water and dissolved substances from the blood out into the tissues. Also substances such as oxygen, carbon dioxide, glucose and urea can diffuse between the blood and the tissues.

B7.7 Workout

1 I've got tennis elbow. Extra **synovial** fluid in the joint is making it painful.
My knee hurts. The bones are rubbing together because I've damaged the **cartilage** at the ends of the bones.
I've sprained my ankle. I overstretched the **ligaments** when I fell.
My arm bone has come out of its socket. The joint is **dislocated**.

2 Gentle exercise/straightening, and flexing the ankle joint/stretching the muscles.

3 **a** F **b** F **c** T **d** F **e** T **f** F **g** T

4

The trainer's question.	Why she asked the question
How much exercise do you normally do?	As a base-line to find out how fit you are likely to be and the level of exercise you should start at.
Do you smoke?	Because smoking affects health and fitness. Extra exercise may stress the body. Smoking can increase the problem.
Do you drink alcohol and if so, how much?	Drinking alcohol also affects health and fitness. It also affects reaction time which is important in many events.
Are you taking any medicines?	Medicines can also affect your health and fitness. The fact that you are taking a medicine tells the trainer that there may be a health issue that he or she needs to know about when devising your training programme.
Is there a family history of heart disease?	This helps to assess your risk of heart disease. It is part of the assessment of your heart health.

B7.7 GCSE-style questions

1 a To find out if there are any health and lifestyle factors that will affect his training.
To find out if there are any lifestyle factors that he should be encouraged to change.
b Do you smoke?
Do you drink alcohol?
Are you taking any medicines?
How much exercise do you do now?
Is there anyone in your family with heart disease or who died of heart disease?
c To find out what has changed./To assess his progress.
To help him to decide on changes to the training programme.
d Lots of possible answers, for example:
Ask about any reduction in symptoms and about any side-effects of the treatment.
Blood tests such as checking for lowered cholesterol.
e Lots of possible answers, for example:
The programme turned out to be too easy or too difficult.
The person had an injury and could therefore do certain forms of exercise.

H **2 a** To remind himself of Simon's answers. As a base-line against which to measure Simon's progress.
b Another fitness trainer may take over Simon's training permanently or during holidays. The trainer may want a second opinion about an aspect of Simon's training.

H **c** It is fairer if conditions such as time of day are the same for each test. Drinking coffee raises the pulse rate. The trainer needs to compare pulse rate under the same conditions over time.

3 a Dislocations (bones out of joint), torn ligaments, torn tendons.
b The joint will be painful and swollen, red or bruised looking and you will find walking difficult.
c Use ice to slow blood flow and reduce pain. Compress using a bandage to reduce swelling. Elevate - raise to reduce blood flow and drain fluid.
d Doing the correct exercises can get the joint moving more quickly. It can also strengthen it to reduce the risk of further injury. Massage can help to stretch or loosen the muscles.

4 a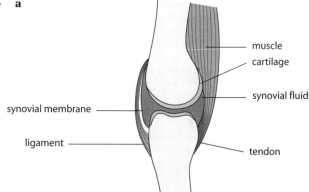

b i Ligaments need to be elastic so that bones can move.

ii Tendons need to be inelastic so that contraction of muscles moves bones rather than stretching tendons.
c Because muscles can move bones at a joint only by contraction. When one muscle of an antagonistic pair contracts, the other muscle relaxes.

Index